The auditorium/dance hall inside Holy Trinity College, Dallas, Texas.
Courtesy of DeAndreis-Rosati Memorial Archives, DePaul University Special Collections, Chicago, IL

TABLE OF CONTENTS

Contributors to this Issue 5

Sisters and Smallpox: The Daughters of Charity as Advocates
For the Sick Poor in Nineteenth-Century Los Angeles
  Kristine Ashton Gunnell, Ph.D. 9

Indifference as the Freedom of Heart: The Spiritual Fruit of Apostolic
Mysticism – Christian, Confucian, and Daoist Cases –
  Sung-Hae Kim, S.C 27

A Challenge to Napoleon: The Defiance of the Daughters of Charity
  Elisabeth Charpy, D.C.. 47
  Translated by Clara Orban, Ph.D., and Edward R. Udovic, C.M.

Saint Louise de Marillac's Uncle: Louis XIII's Garde des Sceaux,
Michel de Marillac (1560-1632)
  Donald A. Bailey, Ph.D. 91

Pictures from the Past: The First University of Dallas
  Essay by Stafford Poole, C.M. 105

Newsnotes 119

© COPYRIGHT DEPAUL UNIVERSITY
VINCENTIAN STUDIES INSTITUTE
VOL. XXX, NO. 2

Contributors to this Issue

DONALD A. BAILEY, Ph.D., taught at the University of Winnipeg, Manitoba, Canada, from 1969 to 2005. In both peer-reviewed journals and daily newspapers, he has published on early Bourbon France, early modern political thought (especially on Locke and Rousseau), the fortunes of French-Canadian cultural rights (language, faith, education, land rights), and Unitarian Universalist theology. His transcription and scholarly edition of *La Vie de Michel de Marillac (1560-1632): Garde des Sceaux de France Sous Louis XIII*, by Nicolas Lefèvre, sieur de Lezeau (Quebec: les Presses de l'Université Laval, 2007), 724 pp., 19 ill., has been well-received. Dr. Bailey recently published a thirty-page booklet entitled, *Music: The Essential Component in Education* (Winnipeg: University of Winnipeg Press, 2010).

SISTER ELISABETH CHARPY, D.C., practiced as a nurse at the hospital of Angers, France, and was director of the School of Nursing at this hospital from 1964 to 1973. She headed the journal *Echoes of the Company* from 1982 to 1989, and it was during this time that she published *Sainte Louise de Marillac: Écrits Spirituels* (Paris: Filles de la Charité, 1983). Since then she has devoted herself to studying the life and spirituality of Louise de Marillac. Notable publications, in French, include: *Contre vents et marées* (Paris: Filles de la Charité, 1988); *Un chemin de sainteté* (Paris: Filles de la Charité, 1988); *La Compagnie aux origines, Documents* (Filles de la Charité, 1989); *Petite vie de Louise de Marillac* (Desclée de Brouwer, 1991); *Louise de Marillac, un feu dévorant, présentation de textes* (Desclée de Brouwer, 1994); *Spiritualité de Louise de Marillac, itinéraire d'une femme* (Desclée de Brouwer, 1995); *Prier 15 jours avec Louise de Marillac* (Nouvelle Cité, 2006); and *Prier 15 jours avec Catherine Labouré* (Nouvelle Cité, 2010). Notable English translations of her works include: *At Prayer with Louise de Marillac* (France: Éditions du Signe, 1995); *A Way to Holiness* (Dublin: Mount Salus Press, 1989); and the *Spiritual Writings of Louise de Marillac* (New York: New City Press, 1991).

KRISTINE ASHTON GUNNELL, Ph.D., completed her doctorate in May 2010 at Claremont Graduate University. She received an M.A. in History from the University of Michigan in 2001, and a B.A. in History from Brigham Young University in 1999. Broadly construed, Dr. Gunnell's research examines the interactions of race, religion, and gender in the construction of urban spaces in the American West. Her dissertation, "The Daughters of Charity and the Development of Social Welfare in Los Angeles, 1856-1927," investigates the ethnic and religious cooperation that surrounded the development of health care and social services in nineteenth-century Los Angeles.   Dr. Gunnell received a research grant from the Vincentian Studies Institute in 2008, and she is currently working on a book project about the history of St. Vincents' Hospital in Los Angeles. Kristine Ashton Gunnell grew up in Bountiful, Utah. She and her husband currently live in a suburb of Los Angeles, and she teaches American history at Claremont McKenna College.

SISTER SUNG-HAE KIM, S.C., is a professor emeritus in the Department of Religious Studies, Sogang University in Seoul, Korea. Sister Sung-Hae presently serves as a general councilor for the Sisters of Charity of Seton Hill at the Generalate in Chicago. After entering the Sisters of Charity of Seton Hill in 1965, Sister received her final vows in 1972. She went on to earn her Th.D. in the History of Religions from Harvard University in 1981. Kim has had numerous articles published — including "The Charism of Charity in East Asian Culture: Reinterpretation of the Spirit of Simplicity, Humility, and Charity" in *Vincentian Heritage* 18:2 — and counts the following titles among books she has authored: *Understanding the History of Religion*; *Primitive Confucianism: A Hermeneutical Approach to the Analects, Mencius, Hsun Tzu*; and she recently co-edited *Monasticism, Buddhist and Christian: The Korean Experience* (Louvain Theological and Pastoral Monographs 38, Peeters, 2008).

REVEREND STAFFORD POOLE, C.M., has been a member of the Vincentian Community since 1947 and a priest since 1956. He holds a master of arts degree in Spanish literature (1958) and a doctorate in history (1961), both from Saint Louis University. He was a founding member of the Secrétariat International d'Études Vincentiennes and the Vincentian Studies Institute. His most recent publications are *Religion in New Spain*, co-edited with Susan Schroeder (University of New Mexico Press, 2007); *Our Lady of Guadalupe*, trans. with Louise Burkhart and Barry Sell, volume 2 of the Nahuatl Theater Project (University of Oklahoma Press, 2006, to be included in the same press's *Aztecs on Stage*); *The Guadalupan Controversies in Mexico* (Stanford University Press, 2006); *Juan de Ovando: Governing the Spanish Empire in the Reign of Philip II* (University of Oklahoma Press, 2004). Forthcoming in 2011 are a second, revised edition of *Pedro Moya de Contreras: Catholic Reform and Royal Power in New Spain* (University of Oklahoma Press), a Spanish translation of the same (Colegio de Michoacán, Zamora, Mexico), and an entry on religion in colonial Mexico for the *Cambridge History of Religion in the Americas*.

Sisters and Smallpox:
The Daughters of Charity as Advocates
For the Sick Poor in Nineteenth-Century
Los Angeles

By

Kristine Ashton Gunnell, Ph.D.

On 6 January 1856, six Daughters of Charity appeared in the plaza of Los Angeles. Led by Sister Mary Scholastica Logsdon, D.C., five of the sisters traveled from the motherhouse of the American province in Emmitsburg, Maryland. Accompanying Bishop Thaddeus Amat, C.M., in October 1855, these women sailed from New York to Panama, crossed the isthmus via the recently completed railroad, and continued up the coast to San Francisco on the steamer *John L. Stephens*. Sister Corsina McKay, D.C., joined the band in San Francisco, and after a month's respite the sisters completed the final leg of the journey to Los Angeles. Arriving unexpectedly, no one met them at San Pedro and the sisters accepted a ride to town from a fellow passenger. Sister Scholastica remembered that shortly after their arrival, "a good, aged, Father came in puffing and blowing and signed for us to follow him."[1] He escorted them to the home of Ygnacio and Ysabel del Valle, who hosted the sisters until the bishop returned from San Gabriel two days later. In the following months, the Daughters of Charity opened the Los Angeles Charitable Institute, which consisted of a school, an orphanage, and an infirmary for the impoverished sick.

In the last decade, a scholarly interest has re-emerged in the influence of "vowed women" (to use Sioban Nelson's term) in American history, including members of active religious communities like the Daughters of Charity. Nelson and Barbra Mann Wall write about Catholic nursing communities, while Maureen Fitzgerald, Dorothy Brown, and Elizabeth McKeown explore the influence of Irish Catholic nuns on social welfare practices in New York City. While several scholars have discussed the experiences of Catholic sisters in the nineteenth-century American West, the interactions of gender, religion, and culture in this region deserve further

---

[1] Mary Scholastica Logsdon, D.C., to Francis Burlando, C.M., Los Angeles, 17 January 1856, in *Daughters of Charity in the City of Angels: A Compilation of Their Early Writings* (Los Altos Hills, California: Daughters of Charity, Province of the West, Seton Provincialate, 2008). Sister Scholastica (1814-1902) joined the community in 1839. She served in New York City, Emmitsburg, MD, and Natchez, MS, before starting the mission in Los Angeles in 1856. Daughters of Charity, Consolidated Database (10-0), Archives St. Joseph's Provincial House, Emmitsburg, Maryland (ASJPH). Consulted at the Daughters of Charity, Province of the West, Seton Provincialate, 21 July and 4 December 2008.

evaluation.[2] Building on the work of Michael Engh, S.J., Anne M. Butler, and others, my research analyzes the social, political, and economic relationships cultivated by the Daughters of Charity to establish and maintain charitable institutions that served the poor in Los Angeles. The Daughters of Charity were among the first to establish houses on the Pacific Coast. At the invitation of the newly-appointed bishops in California, the community established orphanages in San Francisco in 1852, Los Angeles in 1856, and Santa Barbara in 1858.[3] By 1861, the sisters in Los Angeles expanded their charitable works to include an orphanage, a hospital, and a seminary to train new recruits. In this article, I particularly wish to focus on the sisters' role as advocates for the sick poor during the smallpox epidemics in the late nineteenth century.

---

[2] Examples of recent literature include Dorothy M. Brown and Elizabeth McKeown, *The Poor Belong to Us: Catholic Charities and American Welfare* (Cambridge, MA: Harvard University Press, 1997); Maureen Fitzgerald, *Habits of Compassion: Irish Catholic Nuns and the Origins of New York's Welfare System, 1830-1920* (Urbana: University of Illinois Press, 2006); Suellen M. Hoy, *Good Hearts: Catholic Sisters in Chicago's Past* (Urbana: University of Illinois Press, 2006); Sioban Nelson, *Say Little, Do Much: Nurses, Nuns, and Hospitals in the Nineteenth Century* (Philadelphia: University of Pennsylvania Press, 2001); Barbra Mann Wall, *Unlikely Entrepreneurs: Catholic Sisters and the Hospital Marketplace, 1865-1925* (Columbus: Ohio State University Press, 2005). Mary Ewens' now classic work provides a framework for Catholic sisters' expansion into the west, and Coburn and Smith's analysis illustrates nuns' activities in what is now considered the Midwest. See Carol Coburn and Martha Smith, *Spirited Lives: How Nuns Shaped Catholic Culture and American Life, 1836-1920* (Chapel Hill, N.C.: University of North Carolina Press, 1999); Mary Ewens, *The Role of the Nun in Nineteenth-century America* (New York: Arno Press, 1978). As for the Daughters of Charity specifically, Daniel Hannefin, D.C., has written an overall history of the community in the United States, and both Michael Engh, S.J., and Msgr. Francis J. Weber include chapters about the sisters' experiences in Los Angeles in their books. Additionally, Anne M. Butler analyzed the sisters' experiences in Virginia City, Nevada, and has also written an overview of Catholic sisters in the American West. Martha Libster and Betty Ann McNeil, D.C., analyze the sisters' holistic approach to nineteenth-century health care in *Enlightened Charity*. See Anne M. Butler, "Mission in the Mountains: The Daughters of Charity in Virginia City," in *Comstock Women: The Making of a Mining Community*, ed. Ronald M. James and C. Elizabeth Raymond (Reno: University of Nevada Press, 1998); Anne M. Butler, "The Invisible Flock: Catholicism and the American West," in *Catholicism in the American West: A Rosary of Hidden Voices*, ed. Roberto R. Treviño, Richard V. Francaviglia, and Anne M. Butler (College Station: Published for the University of Texas at Arlington by Texas A&M University Press, 2007); Michael E. Engh, S.J., *Frontier Faiths: Church, Temple, and Synagogue in Los Angeles, 1846-1888* (Albuquerque: University of New Mexico Press, 1992); Daniel Hannefin, D.C., *Daughters of the Church: A Popular History of the Daughters of Charity in the United States, 1809-1987* (Brooklyn, New York: New City Press, 1989); Msgr. Francis J. Weber, *California's Reluctant Prelate; The Life and Times of Right Reverend Thaddeus Amat, C.M. (1811-1878)* [Los Angeles: Dawson Book Shop, 1964]; Martha M. Libster and Betty Ann McNeil, D.C., *Enlightened Charity: The Holistic Nursing Care, Education, and Advices Concerning the Sick of Sister Matilda Coskery (1799-1870)* [Golden Apple Publications, 2009].

[3] The Sisters of Loretto also opened Our Lady of Light Academy in Santa Fe in 1852, and the Sisters of Providence founded an orphanage and school in Vancouver, Washington, in 1856. George C. Stewart, *Marvels of Charity: A History of American Sisters and Nuns* (Huntington, IN: Our Sunday Visitor, 1994), 116-118, 148-150.

Catholic sisters played an instrumental role in establishing social welfare services throughout the west, which in turn helped to incorporate these newly-conquered territories into the social, political, and economic structures of the nation. The sisters' schools, orphanages, and hospitals served dual purposes. First, the sisters responded to the needs of the Catholic population in the new territories of the western United States. Secondly, the sisters offered physical and spiritual comfort to all those in need, regardless of religious background. Since the sisters provided the first, and often only, orphanages and hospitals in many isolated western towns, their charitable activities often facilitated local cooperation between Catholics, Protestants, and Jews. In Los Angeles, the Daughters of Charity acted as intermediaries between various religious and cultural groups, bringing together Spanish-Mexican *rancheros*, Jewish merchants, and American politicians in a common cause to alleviate the suffering of poor orphans and the sick. As the key provider of social services in the city before 1880, the sisters became major advocates for improving the treatment of the poor. While class and racial biases encouraged the perpetuation of inhumane conditions in American almshouses, the rules and traditions of the Daughters of Charity required that the poor be treated with "compassion, gentleness, cordiality, respect, and devotion."[4] This approach challenged the derogatory stereotypes associated with the "unworthy poor," and the sisters constantly had to nurture their relationships with benefactors to ensure that they had the resources to adequately meet the needs of the poor men, women, and children in their care.

Caring for the sick poor had been part of the mission of the Daughters of Charity since the community was organized by Vincent de Paul and Louise de Marillac in 1633. However, the sisters' hospital work was rarely funded solely through private donations. Reflecting American social welfare practices that tended to combine public and private efforts, the sisters often partnered with local governments to provide hospital care for impoverished residents during the nineteenth century. After 1855, the California legislature increasingly defined caring for the indigent sick as a county responsibility, and the Los Angeles County Board of Supervisors contracted with the sisters

---

[4] "Common Rules of the Company of Sisters of Charity Called Servants of the Sick Poor Which They Must Keep to Perform Their Duty Well by the Grace of God," in Pierre Coste, C.M., ed., *Vincent de Paul: Correspondence, Conferences, Documents*, ed. and trans. by Jacqueline Kilar, D.C., Marie Poole, D.C., *et al*, 1-11, 13a & 13b (New York: New City Press, 1985-2008), 13b: 151. Hereafter cited as *CCD*.

to provide nursing, food, and housing for impoverished patients in 1858.[5] This arrangement suited both parties for the better part of two decades. However, working with the county thrust the sisters into the political realm. Continually facing tight county budgets and public reluctance to provide for the "unworthy poor," the sisters had to become advocates for their patients, ensuring that they had enough funds to meet patients' needs. At times, this meant that the sisters had to act in subtle, yet still very political ways.

Sisters' Hospital

In Los Angeles, the sisters' hospital began informally at the Charitable Institute (*Institución Caritativa*), the sisters' orphanage and school. Shortly after their arrival, the sisters began nursing sick children and others whom the priests placed in their care. In her memoir, Sister Angelita Mombrado, D.C., recounts the beginning of hospital work in the city: "One day Father [Blaise Raho] came to our house and said he had a very sick man for us to take care of. Sister Ann said, 'Father, where can we put a sick man? We have hardly room for ourselves.' He said that we must find a corner as the man had to be cared for or he would die."[6] Sister Ann Gillen, D.C., cleared out the gardener's shed, and the sisters took the man into their care. By nursing patients at the institute, the Los Angeles sisters continued the mission of the Daughters of Charity to care for the sick poor.

When the opportunity presented itself, the sisters expanded their health services. With financial support from the Los Angeles County Board of Supervisors, the Daughters of Charity opened the first hospital in Southern California. Beginning in a rented adobe in May 1858, the sisters expanded the institution twice, moving to larger facilities in October 1858 and January 1861. Although the sisters owned and managed the Los Angeles Infirmary

---

[5] Theodore H. Hittell, *The General Laws of the State of California from 1850 to 1864, Inclusive*, 2 vols. (San Francisco: H.H. Bancroft and Company, 1865), pars. 3673-3685, pp. 533-534. For a discussion of California's early social welfare practices, see Jacobus tenBroek, "California's Welfare Law — Origins and Development," *California Law Review* 45:3 (1957).

[6] Angelita Mombrado, D.C., "Remembrance of My Youth," in *Daughters of Charity in the City of Angels* (Los Altos Hills, California: Daughters of Charity, Province of the West, Seton Provincialate, 2006), 21. Sister Mombrado (1833-1923) decided to join the community in 1855 when she accepted Bishop Thaddeus Amat's invitation to come to California. Even though she was inexperienced at the time, Sr. Mombrado's ability to speak Spanish was invaluable as she assisted in starting the sisters' missions in Los Angeles (1856) and Santa Barbara (1858). Ann Gillen, D.C. (1818-1902) joined the community in 1840 and served in several orphan asylums before coming to Los Angeles. Notably, at that time Sister Ann was the only sister in Los Angeles who had formal experience working in a hospital — in 1849, she served at Mount Hope, the sisters' general hospital and mental health facility near Baltimore, Maryland. This was likely the reason Sister Scholastica placed her in charge of the hospital. See Consolidated Database (10-0), ASJPH.

The adobe, circa 1858, located on Spring Street.
Courtesy of St. Vincent Medical Center, Historical Conservancy, Los Angeles, CA

(commonly known as County Hospital or Sisters' Hospital), the county provided a majority of its funding.[7] The sisters constructed an institution consistent with the Vincentian heritage of quality care for the poor, but they constantly had to negotiate the cultural and economic pressures posed by limited county finances and supervisors' class biases. As happened elsewhere in the country, Angelenos' Christian charity was often tinged with disdain for the poor, labeling the indigent sick as lazy and dependent, burdens on society. In contrast, the Daughters of Charity pursued hospital work as a way to practice the virtues of humility, simplicity, and charity, while honoring their commitment to serve the poor.[8]

The Los Angeles Infirmary represents the benefits of public-private collaborations to provide for the indigent sick in the nineteenth-century American West. In 1855, the California legislature authorized the collection of passenger fees for a state hospital fund. These funds would then be proportionately distributed to each county according to population, as recorded by the 1855 state census. The legislature designated these funds

---

[7] The hospital founded by the Daughters of Charity in Los Angeles has had several different names. They include an informal infirmary at the *Institución Caritativa* (1856-1858), the Los Angeles County Hospital (1858-1878), Los Angeles Infirmary (1869-1918), St. Vincent's Hospital (1918-1974), and St. Vincent Medical Center (1974-present). In practice, however, the institution was commonly referred to as Sisters' Hospital until the twentieth century.

[8] "Common Rules," *CCD*, 13b: 148.

for treatment of the indigent sick and also authorized boards of supervisors to levy taxes for a county hospital fund, as long as the tax was less than one quarter of one percent.[9] In response to the new law, in July of 1855, the Los Angeles County Board of Supervisors established a sub-committee to better manage the expenses for the county's indigent sick. At the time of treatment, the Committee of Health approved individual applications for county support. Doctors, pharmacists, and boarding house owners then submitted their approved expenses quarterly to the Board of Supervisors to receive payment. Notably, prescriptions had to be submitted in English, and the county physician had to be a "regular graduate" from a recognized medical school.[10] Since the county did not have a hospital, Doctors John S. Griffin and Thomas Foster treated approved patients in private boarding houses. The boarding house owner also submitted bills for food, housing, and nursing care to the county.

The 1855 bill represented part of the Americanization process in the state. The law required that counties hire "regular graduates" as physicians, thereby endorsing scientific medicine and refusing to legitimize midwives, *curanderas*, and homeopathic physicians by paying them with state funds. Requiring prescriptions to be submitted in English also reflected efforts to Americanize local government. These moves illustrate American ascendancy in state government, the application of eastern ideas of social responsibility for the poor, and tensions over the professionalization of medicine which occurred throughout the country. Notably, legal scholar Jacobus tenBroek argues that the 1855 law represented an adaptation of eastern poor laws to California's social conditions. Unlike eastern laws, the California law made no stipulations about residency requirements or family responsibility. Since relatively few American miners came with their families, few men had wives, mothers, or sisters to care for them at home. Nor would these mostly single men have families nearby to pay for their care. And although counties often imposed residency requirements to receive aid, the law implied that counties who accepted state funding would also be responsible for non-residents. The 1855 law was attuned to the social and political conditions of California. Lest we forget, single American-born men voted. This system was primarily designed for them; the miners, laborers, and merchants who fell victim to illness or misfortune.

---

[9] Hittell, *General Laws*, pars. 3674-3681, pp. 533-534.

[10] Supervisors John G. Downey, David Lewis, and Stephen C. Foster were appointed as the Committee of Health, and Doctors John S. Griffin and Thomas Foster attended county patients. Minutes, 7 July 1855, Book 1 (1852-1855), 225-26. Los Angeles County Board of Supervisors Records, Historical Board Minutes, Box 1, Executive Office of the Los Angeles County Board of Supervisors, Los Angeles (LACBS).

The arrival of the Daughters of Charity provided an opportunity for the Los Angeles County Board of Supervisors to engage in a more institutionalized approach to its social welfare services. The sisters' reputation as compassionate, skilled nurses allowed the supervisors to improve health care services and to streamline county financial affairs. Instead of paying several boarding house owners for treatment of the sick, the supervisors would only deal with one institution, and they could better regulate who qualified for services. The benefits to a county-funded hospital included better care, an improved reputation for the city, and hopefully similar or lower costs. While the financial savings did not materialize, the county did receive better services. Since the state government never provided enough funding to meet the need, public-private collaborations proved the best solution to offer health care to the poor in the 1850s and 1860s. California ultimately relied upon a combination of private philanthropy, religious organizations, and government funding to care for the indigent sick. The Daughters of Charity fit perfectly into this matrix of nineteenth-century health care.

Besides providing ongoing care for the county's sick at the Los Angeles Infirmary, the Daughters of Charity also collaborated with city officials in facing public health emergencies during periodic smallpox epidemics in the 1860s, 1870s, and 1880s. Following California's patterns for the distribution of public health responsibilities, the City Council — not the County Board of Supervisors — took the lead in combating the epidemics. The council turned to churches and private charity organizations for additional support. For example, the Daughters of Charity volunteered to staff the pest house, or quarantine hospital, during the smallpox epidemics of 1862-1863, 1868-1869, 1876-1877, 1884, and 1887. The Hebrew Benevolent Society also raised funds to provide food for afflicted families.[11] In so doing, public and private entities combined their efforts to meet the needs of health crises that threatened the entire community. By 1877, the smallpox epidemic posed a significant challenge to the city's reputation as a "healthful place." Striving to protect their bottom line, businessmen pressured city officials to take a more comprehensive approach to public health. But for their part, the Daughters of Charity remained focused on improving the quality of health services for the poor, many of whom suffered from government inefficiency and neglect.

---

[11] Engh, *Frontier Faiths*, 80-82, 147-148.

Containing Disease: American Approaches to Public Health before 1870

In the mid-nineteenth century, American approaches to public health reflected popular understandings of the nature of infectious disease, political attitudes that supported limited government intervention, and cultural tensions regarding social welfare provision for the poor. As historians Suellen Hoy and Jane Eliot Sewell explain, medical theorists remained split over the causes of infectious disease. In *Chasing Dirt*, Hoy argues that many Americans blamed "Filth, usually in the form of noxious odors or 'miasmas' arising from decomposing organic wastes... for epidemics of cholera, yellow fever, and typhoid as well as typhus, scarlet fever, and diphtheria."[12] If filth caused disease, then sanitarians believed that city cleansing campaigns could prevent it. However, Sewell explains that other theorists, called contagionists, "thought that infectious diseases were caused by specific contagious elements or organisms."[13] In the face of competing theories, most cities compromised by combining city cleansing with efforts to isolate suspected sources of contagion. During epidemics, authorities used sanitary regulations and quarantine efforts to halt the spread of contagious disease.

A tradition of limited government intervention also influenced American approaches to public health in the nineteenth century. As Sewell explains, early nineteenth-century officials often deemed ongoing public health actions as unnecessary due to cultural assumptions that "Americans were naturally tougher, healthier hybrids of their inbred, confined European ancestors."[14] Only unusual threats required intervention, and many believed that government action, when taken, should be temporary. Americans tolerated restrictive measures, and the higher taxes resulting from increased government expenditures, as necessary responses to perceived crises. But as the threat subsided, public support for ongoing preventative measures waned. Baltimore, for example, organized street cleaning campaigns, mandated quarantines, set up temporary hospitals, and recruited emergency nursing staff (including the Sisters of Charity) during the cholera outbreak of 1832. However, as the immediate threat subsided, politicians cut funding for sanitation and hospital services, leaving the city unprepared for another

---

[12] Suellen M. Hoy, *Chasing Dirt: The American Pursuit of Cleanliness* (New York: Oxford University Press, 1995), 61.

[13] Jane Eliot Sewell, *Medicine in Maryland: The Practice and the Profession, 1799-1999* (Baltimore: Johns Hopkins University Press, 1999), 122.

[14] Sewell, *Medicine in Maryland*, 117-129, quote on 118. See also Charles E. Rosenberg, *The Cholera Years: The United States in 1832, 1849, and 1866* (Chicago: University of Chicago Press, 1962), 14-16; Barbara Gutmann Rosenkrantz, *Public Health and the State: Changing Views in Massachusetts, 1842-1936* (Cambridge: Harvard University Press, 1972), 4.

outbreak in 1848.[15] By responding to crises as needed, Baltimore and other cities developed an ad hoc approach to public health. Temporary government intervention suited American political traditions — and city budgets — until more comprehensive public health reform started to take hold in the 1880s.

Similar notions of frontier "toughness," combined with limited government resources, encouraged Californians to adopt the same ad hoc approach to public health during the mid-nineteenth century. During smallpox outbreaks, Los Angeles officials developed a three-pronged approach to halt the spread of the disease. First, the city appointed health inspectors to find and report smallpox cases. The inspectors posted yellow quarantine flags in front of patients' homes, warning the neighborhood of the presence of the disease and restricting the movements of household members. Second, the city opened a quarantine hospital, or "pest house," to treat indigent patients who could not afford to pay physicians' fees. Patients without family members to provide nursing care were also sent to the pest house. Third, the city embarked on vaccination campaigns, offering smallpox vaccinations free of charge to city residents. These strategies worked with varying degrees of effectiveness during the periodic epidemics of the 1860s, 1870s, and 1880s.

As in Baltimore, Angelenos expected government intervention to be temporary. When smallpox first appeared during the winter of 1862, the city appointed a board of health and Mayor Damien Marchessault hired inspectors to canvass the city and report every case that appeared in Los Angeles. Marchessault also purchased a "pest house" four miles outside of town and asked the Daughters of Charity to nurse patients there.[16] One sister recalled that when Sister Scholastica and Sister Ann went to inspect the pest house, they found "patients lying pell-mell on the floor, suffering in every way… Some becoming delirious from fever, would rush out over the patients thickly strewn over the floor."[17] After seeing patients in such a "pitiable condition," the Daughters of Charity agreed to take charge of the pest house, cleaned it up, and began caring for those afflicted with the

---

[15] Sewell, *Medicine in Maryland*, 117-129; Libster and McNeil, *Enlightened Charity*, 64-67.

[16] Engh, *Frontier Faiths*, 81.

[17] "Remarks on Sister Mary Scholastica Logsdon, who died at the Orphan Asylum, Los Angeles, California, U.S., September 9, 1902; 88 Years of Age, 66 of Vocation," *Lives of Our Deceased Sisters* (1903): 113. Because of the nature of the source, there may be some inaccuracies in the account. This comment most likely refers to the 1862-1863 smallpox epidemic, but it is not dated. In general, few sources remain which discuss the 1862-1863 epidemic in detail. The 1903 account asserts that the sisters requested the city move the pest house closer to town, so they might have better access to patients. It also claims that a family moved out of the home to accommodate the pest house. It is unclear whether this request was made in 1862 or 1869, and I have not been able to corroborate this with evidence from other sources.

disease. Although it is likely that relatively few of the deaths occurred at the pest house, approximately two hundred people throughout the county died during the epidemic. However, as reports of the disease dwindled, the board of health requested permission to disband in March 1863. The Common Council agreed, and it is probable they closed the pest house too.[18] Angelenos did not expect the board of health to become a permanent fixture in city government.

Historian Jennifer Koslow notes that the Common Council followed a similar pattern during the epidemics in the winter of 1868 and spring of 1869. Like in other cities, Los Angeles officials used both the contagionist and sanitarian approach to halting the spread of disease. The council appointed a temporary board of health, quarantined patients at home, and hired Dr. Henry S. Orme to administer smallpox vaccinations. Quarantining patients and administering vaccinations appeased the "contagionists," who believed that microscopic organisms caused the disease. But the council also engaged in sanitarian city cleansing efforts by instructing Orme to report public health "nuisances," such as poor sewerage, rotting animal carcasses, and filthy pig sties. The council also mandated that all children had to be vaccinated before attending school, and the city built a new pest house in the fall of 1868.[19] By December of 1868 the number of cases dwindled, however the disease reemerged in May 1869. The Common Council then asked the Daughters of Charity to nurse patients at the pest house, which they did until the epidemic subsided at the end of June. At that time the council dismissed Orme, disbanded the board of health, and closed the pest house.[20] As in 1863, city officials responded to health crises as needed, but did so through a temporary expansion of government authority.

While scientific theories of disease and political support for limited government shaped American public health practices during the nineteenth century, smallpox and other contagious diseases also exacerbated racial and

---

[18] Engh, *Frontier Faiths*, 80-81; George Harwood Phillips, "Indians in Los Angeles, 1781-1875: Economic Integration, Social Disintegration," *The Pacific Historical Review* 49:3 (1980): 448-449. Jennifer L. Koslow, "Public Health," in *The Development of Los Angeles City Government: An Institutional History, 1850-2000*, ed. Hynda Rudd (Los Angeles: City of Los Angeles Historical Society, 2007), 484.

[19] The Daughters of Charity requested the pest house be moved closer to town, although it is not entirely clear whether this was done in 1869 or 1877. According to the 1884 Stevenson map, the pest house was located on Reservoir Street, near Adobe, adjacent to the Hebrew Cemetery. This is approximately the same location that the Common Council deeded to the sisters for "hospital purposes" in 1857. Deed, The Mayor & Common Council of the City of Los Angeles to the Novice Sisters of Charity, 2 May 1857, Binder and Newspaper Copies of History of the Daughters and SVMC, Los Altos, Saint Vincent Medical Center Historical Conservancy, Los Angeles (SVMCHC); "Remarks on Sister Scholastica," 113; H.J. Stevenson, "Map of the City of Los Angeles," 1884, Collection 294, Maps of Los Angeles, the United States, and the World, ca. 1516-, UCLA.

[20] Koslow, "Public Health," 485-487.

class tensions in communities throughout the United States. In 1863 and 1869, smallpox disproportionately affected the Mexican and Native American populations in Los Angeles, and by 1876, the press blamed the "festering filth" in Chinatown for the reemergence of the disease.[21] By labeling Chinatown as the city's "plague spot," historian Natalia Molina argues that the press, and city officials, "assigned responsibility for these conditions to the area's Chinese residents," rather than to the Anglo landlords who ignored sanitary conditions.[22] As they deflected attention from economic exploitation and racial prejudice, Los Angeles officials started to conflate race with poverty and threats to public health. If, as some Angelenos believed, Chinese culture encouraged poor hygiene, opium addiction, and immoral behavior, then Chinese immigrants needed to be controlled and contained as a means to protect public health. As Molina argues, quarantine measures and public health ordinances disproportionately affected people of color in Los Angeles, reinforcing images that portrayed Chinese and Mexican residents as "foreign" and "dangerous" to the American citizenry.

Class biases also shaped public responses to smallpox epidemics. In *The Cholera Years*, Charles Rosenberg explained that many middle-class Americans underreported cholera cases in their families to avoid association with the "shameful disease," assumed to be brought on by the dirty, intemperate, and immoral behavior of the "dishonorable" poor.[23] Sensitive to this image of shame, Los Angeles officials developed a class-based response to the needs of smallpox patients. Middle-class patients could remain in their homes, treated by family members and a private physician, and quarantines for them were not always strictly enforced. However, the health officer unceremoniously scurried poor patients out of town and forced them to endure the humiliation of being treated in the pest house. Like nineteenth-century almshouses, pest houses often suffered from government inefficiency and neglect. Upon her arrival at the Los Angeles pest house in 1887, Sister Veronica Klimkiewicz, D.C., noted that the building was in such a state of disrepair that it was "hardly fit for domestic animals." The city had hired incompetent and unreliable caretakers, for whom "the large pecuniary consideration offered was the principal, if not the only inducement to enter so repulsive a service." Because of the filthy conditions and a reputation for indifferent care, Sister Veronica explained, "As a consequence, none, or very few, who were in circumstances to resist the public pressure that sought to

---

[21] "Chinatown," *Evening Republican*, 3 October 1876; Koslow, "Public Health," 486; Phillips, "Indians in Los Angeles," 448-449.

[22] Natalia Molina, *Fit to be Citizens? Public Health and Race in Los Angeles, 1879-1939* (Berkeley: University of California Press, 2006), 23-30, quote on page 28.

[23] Rosenberg, *The Cholera Years*, 55-57.

force them into such dire isolation, could be induced to leave their homes."[24] Justifiably, most Angelenos avoided entering the quarantine hospital for fear of living in squalor, and thus hastening death.

Building on antebellum trends that contained the deviant, depraved, or simply the poor into public institutions, Californians started to regulate, isolate, and contain racial minorities as "threats to the health of the community" in the late nineteenth century. Although often underfunded and understaffed, historian Nayan Shah argues that public health officials held considerable "legal authority to regulate property and people's conduct."[25] As made evident during the smallpox epidemics, class and racial biases often mediated the application of this authority, and continuing disdain for the poor — especially those afflicted with contagious diseases — led to inadequate funding for facilities, nursing care, and sanitation. Despite these prejudices, the Daughters of Charity engaged with city officials to improve conditions for the sick poor by nursing individuals without regard to race, creed, or class. The sisters thereby challenged the deeply ingrained notions of inequality which dominated society in the nineteenth-century American West.

The Pest House and the Daughters of Charity

As a part of emergency efforts to halt the epidemics, city officials turned to the Daughters of Charity to provide nursing care to the poor in the city-owned pest house. At the height of each epidemic, Sister Scholastica Logsdon agreed to send two or three sisters to take charge of the pest house.[26] Like at the Los Angeles Infirmary, the sisters negotiated a contract to provide nursing care, food, and provisions for smallpox patients, while the city paid

---

[24] Veronica Klimkiewicz, D.C., to Euphemia Blenkinsop, D.C., 20 June 1887, Maryvale Historical Collection, Maryvale, Rosemead, California. Copy consulted at SVMCHC, March 2009. Sister Veronica (1837-1930) joined the community in 1854 and served in twelve of the sisters' institutions (schools, orphan asylums, and hospitals) in the eastern United States before coming to the Los Angeles Infirmary in 1884. Consolidated Database (10-0), ASJPH.

[25] Nayan Shah, *Contagious Divides: Epidemics and Race in San Francisco's Chinatown* (Berkeley: University of California Press, 2001), 6.

[26] Sister Ann Gillen and several other sisters may have assisted at the pest house in the winter of 1862-1863. Sisters Phileta McCarthy, D.C., and Margaret Weber, D.C., supervised the pest house in May 1869. Sisters Mary Ellen Downey, D.C., and Frances Xavier Schauer, D.C., treated patients at the pest house in the winter of 1876-1877, and Sister Veronica Klimkiewicz recorded her experiences in the pest house in 1887. See notes for her letter below. The *Los Angeles Herald* states that Sisters Josephine, Xavier, and Veronica served in the pest house in 1887. This likely means Sister Josephine Leddy, D.C., and Sister Xavier Schauer. "The Smallpox," *Los Angeles Herald*, 9 March 1887. In 1879, Sister Phileta McCarthy became the sister servant in Santa Barbara. Engh, *Frontier Faiths*, 80-82, 147-148.

for medicine, clothing, and bedding. The city also agreed that the sisters could manage the facility according to their rules and traditions. The City Council needed the Daughters of Charity to lend their angelic reputation to the pest house in part to convince more patients to enter isolation and thereby slow the advance of the epidemic. As Sister Veronica later explained, city officials hoped "few would refuse to go where such ministrations as theirs were offered."[27] But the sisters agreed to step in *only* if the city provided improved facilities and adequate funding for patient care. Knowing this, the city council often delayed hiring the Daughters of Charity as long as was possible, presumably to avoid spending money unnecessarily on the "unworthy poor." They only accepted the sisters' service when the disease reached truly "epidemic" proportions. By insisting on "suitable conditions" at the pest house, the Daughters of Charity used their political leverage to improve the quality of care for the sick poor. The sisters also continued their spiritual mission to alleviate the suffering of those in need.

Pest house conditions were deplorable under the city's management. In 1877, patients included Irish immigrants, Mexicans, Indians, and others without families to care for them.[28] Even though the pest house was isolated on the outskirts of town, few Angelenos wanted to risk contracting smallpox by delivering supplies, washing laundry, or nursing patients. The temporary nature of such an emergency also provided little incentive for council members to invest in improving pest house conditions. Before the sisters arrived, the facility reeked with filth, fleas and lice covered the bed linens, and some patients "were at times a literal mass of corruption with maggots crawling from their ears and nose."[29] Unsurprisingly, few smallpox patients chose to be treated in the pest house. Only one-quarter of the 360 cases reported in 1876 and 1877 received treatment at the facility.[30] Few sick Angelenos risked entering the pest house, perhaps fearing social disparagement, but more likely because they feared the disease itself would worsen given the lack of care provided by the city.

Political pressure from the Grand Jury, and an angry citizen's committee, forced the city council to take more comprehensive action to

---

[27] Klimkiewicz to Blenkinsop, 20 June 1887.

[28] While under the sisters' management between 25 February and 14 April 1877, thirty of the thirty-eight patients were men. The rosters listed three Indians, with the majority of other patients possessing Spanish or Irish surnames. Pest House Warrants, 20 April 1877. City Treasurer, Bills Paid. Minutes of City Council, Vol. 10, 12, Los Angeles City Archives, Los Angeles, CA.

[29] Klimkiewicz to Blenkinsop, 20 June 1887.

[30] "Health Officer Reports," *Evening Republican*, 20 October 1876 – 20 April 1877; "City Council Minutes," *Evening Republican*, 9 February 1877; "Concilio Comun," *La Crónica*, 13 January 1877; Pest House Warrants, 20 April 1877.

The Sisters' Hospital located on Ann Street, circa 1880.
Courtesy of St. Vincent Medical Center, Historical Conservancy, Los Angeles, CA

safeguard the health of its citizens. After an explosive council meeting, Sister Scholastica sent a message to city hall. On 8 February 1877, she offered "to take charge of a suitable pest house, at the rate of $3 per day for each patient, the Council to furnish physicians and medicines."[31] The sisters agreed to supply all the provisions for the establishment, including wine and liquor, but the city would continue to provide other medicines, bedding, and clothing for patients. Sister Scholastica also required the city to construct a two-story wooden building (eighteen feet square) for the sister-nurses to live in. The city would continue to maintain a wagon and driver for use by the hospital, arrange burials as needed, and patients would not be allowed to bring liquor into the hospital without permission.[32] The sisters' offer was unanimously accepted on 8 February, the council paid nearly two thousand dollars ($1,986) for a new building on 24 February, and the Daughters of Charity likely took charge of the pest house on 25 February 1877.[33] The sisters' presence had an immediate effect. On 2 March, the health officer reported that twenty

---

[31] "City Council Minutes," *Evening Republican*, 9 February 1877.

[32] "Concilio Comun," *La Crónica*, 10 February 1877.

[33] "City Council Minutes," *Evening Republican*, 24 February 1877. The first bills recording payments of three dollars per day per patient began on 25 February, so the sisters must have taken over the pest house around that time. See Pest House Warrants, 20 April 1877.

of the fifty-nine cases of smallpox reported in the city were being treated at the pest house, nearly doubling the percentage of afflicted patients receiving care at the facility.[34] The reputation of the Daughters of Charity had boosted Angelenos' confidence in the city's public health efforts.

In requesting a "suitable pest house," the Daughters of Charity used their political leverage to improve the quality of life for their patients. The sisters only agreed to manage a *suitable* pest house, thus forcing the council to pay for improvements and thereby increasing patients' confidence that they would receive quality care. The sisters also required sizeable funds to cover the cost of treating patients. They requested three dollars in gold per patient per day from the City Council, whereas the County Board of Supervisors only paid seventy-five cents per day for patients at the Los Angeles Infirmary.[35] Under public pressure, the council quickly agreed, despite the extraordinary difference in cost. The council understood that it would be easier to quarantine patients in the pest house under the sisters' care, slowing the spread of the disease and mollifying the council's critics.

But why did the sisters ask for so much more? The sisters did not take a salary either at the pest house or the county hospital, so hazard pay would not factor into the equation. I suspect that the sisters asked for three dollars per day because it more adequately covered rising health care costs than the meager allotment accorded to the Los Angeles Infirmary. As Sister Veronica later noted, the increased subsidy from the City Council allowed the sisters "to minister to [patients'] wants in a manner at once more acceptable

---

[34] On 9 February, the health officer reported fifty-three cases in the city; ten were being treated in the pest house. "City Council Minutes," *Evening Republican*, 9 February 1877. On 2 March, the health officer reported fifty-nine cases in the city; twenty being treated at the pest house. "City Council Minutes," *Evening Republican*, 2 March 1877.

[35] The sisters likely required payment in gold because of the recent economic crisis in Los Angeles. Paul R. Spitzzeri notes that city treasurer J.J. Mellus deposited $23,000 of the city's funds in the Temple and Workman bank early in 1875. Unfortunately, the bank fell victim to the August financial crisis sparked by overspeculation in Nevada's Comstock silver trade. In response to the panic caused by the closure of San Francisco's Bank of California on 26 August 1875, both Los Angeles banks (Farmers' and Merchants' Bank and the Temple and Workman) temporarily closed their doors. Although Farmers' and Merchants' reopened on 1 October, co-founder F.P.F. Temple was unable to quickly secure a loan and he could not reopen Temple and Workman until 6 December 1875. Unfortunately, Elias J. ("Lucky") Baldwin's loan was not enough to save the bank. The Temple and Workman Bank closed permanently on 13 January 1876. According to Spitzzeri, the city likely lost all of its funds. See Paul R. Spitzzeri, *The Workman and Temple Families of Southern California, 1830-1930* (Dallas: Seligson Press, 2008), 159-193, and especially 164 and 184 for the city's connection to the bank failure. While the sisters did not contract with the city to care for smallpox patients until February 1877, the requirement to be paid in gold suggests that there was still some hesitancy on their part concerning the council's ability to pay its bills.

and better calculated to promote their recovery."[36] However, we should also analyze these actions as part of a greater political discourse.

In February 1877, the sisters found themselves in the midst of a movement to deprive them of the contract for the county's charity patients. The Daughters of Charity had cared for charity patients at the Los Angeles Infirmary since 1858. Throughout this time, the Board of Supervisors steadily applied pressure on the sisters to cut costs, and the board reduced their rate to seventy-five cents per patient per day in 1871.[37] Despite smaller revenues, the sisters continued to care for impoverished patients as best they could. Yet the sisters received public criticism for inadequate conditions at the hospital in 1875 and 1876. Noticeably, the critics failed to note that reduced county funding and a negligent county physician lay at the root of these problems. In 1877, the sisters may have requested their three dollar per patient rate in part to illustrate the inadequacy of the county's paltry sum. Although the Daughters of Charity did not engage in public protests or appear personally at city council meetings, I would argue that their request for greater funding did send a political message.

The sisters' actions were not motivated by self-interest, requesting improvements to facilities and ample funding to buy supplies was an act of social advocacy *on behalf of poor patients*. Adequate funding allowed the Daughters of Charity to care for poor patients with respect and dignity, and the sisters were mindful of their roles as advocates for their patients' physical and spiritual comfort. The Daughters clearly understood that the city and county hospitals needed to be economically viable in order to sustain the sisters' spiritual mission. Compassion cannot completely overcome insolvency, and the sisters actively cultivated relationships that facilitated the accomplishment of their spiritual objectives. They understood the political environment they worked in, and they acted in ways to preserve their agency and autonomy, always in an effort to provide the best possible care for the men, women, and children they served. As Sister Veronica noted, "It was a missionary as well as a sanitary work that we were called to do."[38]

The Daughters of Charity served the sick poor as a means to strengthen their own faith and devotion, but they also engaged in this Christian service to encourage others to return to the Catholic fold. Sister Veronica Klimkiewicz happily reported that many of the "coarse, uncouth, and ill-natured" patients were "by their sufferings and by the consolation of Religion, commended to them daily… brought to a better realization of their

---

[36] Klimkiewicz to Blenkinsop, 20 June 1887.

[37] "Hospital Item," *Los Angeles Star*, 7 March 1871.

[38] Klimkiewicz to Blenkinsop, 20 June 1887.

Dated 1910, a postcard portrayal of the Los Angeles Infirmary.
Courtesy of Vincentiana Collection, DePaul University Special Collections, Chicago, IL

spiritual needs and to a nearer communion with God."[39] As with other aspects of their service, spiritual needs came first for the Daughters of Charity. Sister Veronica and her companions placed their trust in Providence, and sought to extend mercy to those who had found none, despite the many experiences Sister Veronica feared "would prove a harrowing scourge for the remainder of life."[40] The Daughters offered spiritual comfort and practical help. They listened to patients, taught spiritual principles, and invited the priest to offer the sacraments. But, the sisters also went to work cleaning the building, replacing the sheets and blankets, and "so changing and transforming the whole house that the Resident Physician said of it, 'what was once a hell has become a paradise since the Sisters took matters in charge.'"[41]

The Daughters of Charity maintained a tradition of courageous self-sacrifice through nursing the sick during epidemics throughout the United States. When others fled, Catholic sisters remained in cities such as Baltimore and New Orleans during the cholera epidemics of 1832 and 1848. Their willingness to risk infection and death did much to soften anti-Catholic attitudes in the United States, and it opened doors for the further expansion

---

[39] *Ibid.*

[40] *Ibid.*

[41] *Ibid.*

of their mission. Along with the sisters' service in the Civil War, the cholera epidemics solidified Catholic sisters' reputation to provide quality nursing and garnered greater support for Catholic hospitals. In Los Angeles, the Daughters of Charity stepped to the fore to provide service during the smallpox epidemics. Their reputation for kind, caring, and effective nursing encouraged sick Angelenos to enter the quarantine hospital, isolating patients and hopefully retarding the spread of the disease. In knowing city officials needed them, the sisters utilized their political leverage to provide the best care possible, insisting that the city improve conditions in the pest house and grant adequate funding for the sick poor.

Indifference as the Freedom of Heart: The Spiritual Fruit of Apostolic Mysticism — Christian, Confucian, and Daoist Cases — [1]

By
Sung-Hae Kim 金勝惠, S.C.

Introduction

I have presented a course entitled "Comparative Mysticism" at Sogang University for the last twenty-five years and my students have commented that it was the flower of all that I taught. That said, I would like to talk not about a flower which is beautiful yet fades away, but a fruit that lasts and nourishes people. The current interest in mysticism today is not only theoretical and practical but ecumenical and cross-cultural in its orientation. The capacity of emotion to add richness and depth to our lives has been recognized. But the quest for more intense feelings of personal intimacy with nature and life, as well as with the divine, has been most authentically realized in the mystical dimension of religious traditions. It is important for us to remember that, "Contrary to many popular images, the mystical religious mode is not extraordinary and is not for reclusive types. As James and others have asserted, there is a mystical dimension in all serious and sincere religion."[2]

The fact that a mystical religious mode of life is neither extraordinary nor reclusive leads us to look at the relationship between apophatic/negative mysticism and kataphatic/positive mysticism. Janet Ruffing points out that there has been a strong bias favoring the apophatic style of mystical experience in mystical literature, and that the kataphatic way is regarded merely as a prelude to the real, true, or most authentic mystical experience.[3] She asserts that "The kataphatic experience is something like looking through an open window at... the divine reality... In the apophatic experience, there is no window, but the same objectless object of attention

---

[1] This paper was originally presented at the *International Conference on Mystical Tradition and Autobiography as the Source of the Multicultural Spirituality in a Global World*, 20-23 October 2008, Sogang University, Seoul, Korea.

[2] *The New Catholic Encyclopedia*, 2nd ed., s.v. "Mysticism" (The Catholic University of America, 2003), 10:116. This recent conclusion modified both Henri Bergson's assertion that true mysticism is exception and John Hick's statement that any firsthand religious experience is mystical experience.

[3] Janet K. Ruffing, RSM, "The World Transfigured: Kataphatic Religious Experience Explored through Qualitative Research Methodology," *Studies in Spirituality* 5 (1995), 232.

is disclosed in a subtle presence/absence."[4] I agree with her assertion that the kataphatic experience of God, which includes symbols, meditation with imagination, incarnation, and natural images, is neither inferior nor simply the prelude to the apophatic experience. However, I would like to stress that the authenticity of both apophatic and kataphatic mysticism should be measured by the resulting purity or freedom of heart – termed "indifference" in Christianity, "absence of private mind"(無私心) in Confucianism, and the "equitable and constant ordinary mind"(平常心) in Daoism.

I will provide three examples, one from each of three religious traditions: Saint Vincent de Paul from seventeenth-century France; Cheng Yi 程頤 from eleventh-century North Song China; and Yin Zhiping 尹志平 from the thirteenth-century Mongol period of China. I chose them because they were passionately social-minded mystics who lived a very active life, leaving a lasting legacy in their respective traditions which continues on in our day.

Vincent de Paul (1581-1660) founded the Congregation of the Mission, an order of priests and brothers committed to the poor (he thought the poor should be the center of the Church) and the spiritual renewal of the Church. In collaboration with Louise de Marillac he also founded the Daughters of Charity, whose apostolic life became the inspiration for the largest number of present-day women religious. Vincent also was the inspiration for numerous social-welfare systems and charitable associations in the Western world. I was fascinated, however, not so much by his vast influence in social-welfare works, but by his pursuit of a pure quality of love or freedom of heart, something he termed the "virtue of indifference."

For the first ten years of his priesthood Vincent was an ambitious, secular man looking for success and good fortune like many ordinary priests of his era in France. His parents sent him to the seminary as an investment, so that he could in return help to improve his family through educating his nephews. A letter to his mother, who lived in the farming village of Pouy near Dax in Southern France, reveals his filial but worldly pursuit of life: "The assurance that Monsieur de Saint-Martin has given me with regard to your good health has gladdened me, as much as the prolonged sojourn which I must necessarily make in this city in order to regain my chances for advancement (which my disasters took from me) grieves me, because I cannot come to render you the services I owe you. But I have such trust in God's grace, that He will bless my efforts and will soon give me the means of an honorable retirement so that I may spend the rest of my days near

---

[4] *Ibid.*, 235.

you."[5] This letter of 17 February 1610, which he wrote at the age of thirty-one, contrasts sharply to the homily he delivered during his last visit to his hometown in 1623 as General Chaplain of the Galleys in Paris and Bordeaux. He celebrated High Mass for villagers and his relatives at the shrine of Our Lady of Buglose, telling them to rid their hearts of any desire to become rich, and to not expect any financial help from him as everything a priest has belongs to God and the poor.[6]

Vincent had experienced a conversion of heart through his acquaintance with two spiritual leaders of the French School in Paris, Pierre de Bérulle and André Duval, and also through his pastoral experience of the poor in the desolate farming estates of Madame de Gondi. André Duval, his life-time confessor, introduced Vincent to *The Rule of Perfection*, written by Benet of Canfield, from which he learned the importance of waiting for God to lead, the truth of not treading on the heels of Providence.[7] As he discovered Jesus in the face of the poor and committed himself to serve them as his masters, he was freed from the desire to become rich and a need to implement self-serving plans. To probe the mystical depth of his emphasis on the virtue of indifference I will use his conferences to the Congregation of the Mission and Daughters of Charity as my primary source.

Cheng Yi 程頤 (1033-1107), one of the founders of Neo-Confucianism, established the theoretical frame for Zhu Xi 朱熹 and pursued learning that enables one to become a sage. In his memorial to the emperor he advised him to avoid mundane pursuits and follow the kingly way: "Your subject humbly suggests that the learning [of the sages] has not been transmitted for a long time. Fortunately, your subject has been able to obtain it from the Classics that have been handed down... because he took upon himself the responsibility for the Way."[8] When he was appointed a lecturer to the emperor in 1086, he taught the lesson of Yan Hui, the disciple of Confucius, who never lost his joy even under impoverished circumstances.[9] Many consider Cheng Yi's emphasis on principle (*li* 理) rigid and especially criticize his austere teaching against the remarriage of widows. However, while reading his commentaries on the *Book*

---

[5] Pierre Coste, C.M., ed., *Vincent de Paul: Correspondence, Conferences, Documents*, ed. and trans. by Jacqueline Kilar, D.C., Marie Poole, D.C., *et al*, 1-11, 13a & 13b (New York: New City Press, 1985-2008), 1:15-16. Hereinafter cited as *CCD*.

[6] José María Román, *St. Vincent de Paul: A Biography*, trans. Joyce Howard, D.C. (London: Melisende, 1999), 159.

[7] *Vincent de Paul and Louise de Marillac: Rules, Conferences, and Writings,* The Classics of Western Spirituality (Vincentian Studies Institute, Paulist Press, 1995), 16.

[8] *RoutledgeCurzon Encyclopedia of Confucianism*, ed. Xinzhong Yao (New York: RoutledgeCurzon, 2003), 1:61.

[9] *Analects of Confucius*, 6:11.

of Changes and the Four Books, I was surprised to find how much emphasis he placed on discernment in changing circumstances. He was much more aware of the real world, which is always fluctuating and open to the Timely Mean (時中), than Zhu Xi, who focused his attention on the unchanging principle.

His strictness with his students, as well as with himself, was due to his keen awareness that there is a constant struggle in the human heart / mind between the principle of Heaven (天理) and human desires (人欲). Since Confucians used to contrast the public mind (公), representing the principle of Heaven, with the private (私), denoting disordered human desires, Cheng Yi discussed extensively the problem of the private mind and how we can cultivate the virtue of benevolence in order to overcome it.[10] My primary sources are the Neo-Confucian anthology, *Reflections on Things at Hand*, and Cheng Yi's *Commentary on the Book of Changes*, which is regarded as one of the most important Confucian interpretations.

Yin Zhiping 尹志平 (1169-1251), was a disciple of Qiu Chuji 丘處機 (whose Daoist pen name was Changchun 長春), the youngest and most famous among the "Seven Perfected Ones" (七眞) of the Complete Perfection Order (*Quanzhen jiao* 全眞教). Founded by Wang Zhe 王嚞, who started the successful reform movement in twelfth-century China, the Complete Perfection Order flourished and continues today as the representative community of Daoist masters, distinguishing itself from the older Daoist sect of Heavenly Masters through its strict celibate lifestyle and practice of inner alchemy. When Changchun was invited by Genghis Khan and honored as an immortal, Yin Zhiping accompanied him, with seventeen other disciples, on their long westward journey (1219-1223).

Yin Zhiping not only succeeded Changchun as the sixth patriarch of his order, but he established the basic principle of integrating inner cultivation (內功) and outer cultivation (外功). In a period of constant war and famine requiring much social work from his order, Yin Zhiping learned from Changchun that inner cultivation through non-action (*wuwei* 無爲), and outer cultivation through action (*youwei* 有爲), are intimately related, and in the end one, because both are based on the Way (*Dao* 道).[11] In fact, non-action can be action when one performs the work without attachment, and

---

[10] For a history of the usage of the term "private" and "private mind" in Confucian tradition, refer to my article, "The Problem of Private Mind," in *People's Religion and the People of Religion* (사람의 종교, 종교의 사람), 서강 종교연구회 엮음, 바오출판사 (2008), 49-88.

[11] 師父曰: 有爲無爲一而已, 於道同也. *The Records of Conferences during the Northern Journey by True Man Qing He* (清和眞人北遊語錄, 中華道藏) [1633] Volume 26, p. 731, section 1. Disciples began to gather his conferences around 1237 and wrote the preface in 1240.

through timely action one can achieve a state of non-action.[12] Therefore he emphasized cultivation of ordinary life, that we should practice moderation and harmony while faced with the emotions of happiness, anger, sadness, and joy. He called this state of mind "Ordinary Mind" (平常心). Yin Zhiping adopted the term from Zen Buddhist circles but he gave it new meaning. He asserted we have to maintain a constant mind while experiencing human feelings: "When we govern our mind and attain the state of equity and constancy; then the Way springs up naturally."[13] Yin Zhiping's conferences given during visitations to various Daoist monasteries in the Northern Region (北遊錄) shed light on his concept of the Ordinary Mind, which integrates contemplation and action into one.

Vincent de Paul preaching about charity. Period etching by Alexandre David.
Image Collection of the Vincentian Studies Institute

---

[12] Zhang Guangbao 張廣保, *Studies on the Mind and Nature of Inner Alchemy in the Complete Perfection Order of Jin and Yuan Period* (金元全眞道「丹心性學) [Beijing: Sanlian Publishers, 1995], 98.

[13] 治其心得至於平常, 則其道自生. *Ibid.*, p. 737, third section.

1. The Virtue of Indifference in the Conferences of Vincent de Paul

Vincent de Paul did not write an autobiography or theoretical treatises on mysticism. Therefore, his conferences to the priests and brothers, and the Daughters of Charity, along with his letters, are the source for his intimate thoughts. While his letters (3,000 preserved) are personal and concrete responses to particular circumstances, his conferences are public and oriented toward the spiritual formation of his male and female communities. Even though he delivered a conference every Friday evening to the Congregation of the Mission only thirty-one, presented during the last three years of his life (1657-1660), are preserved, as Vincent did not like his talks to be recorded. However, we do have 120 conferences (1634-1660) to the Daughters. Louise de Marillac persuaded Vincent that poor country girls without proper theological education needed to read his talks over and over again. His conferences were typically conversations on a subject Vincent announced beforehand. The missioners and Daughters were to contemplate the given theme and share their reflections, at the end of which Vincent would affirm and encourage their thought, offering his own thought which thereby formed the core of the conferences. The themes were varied: explanations on the rules, love and service for the poor, conviction for vocation, total surrender to God, and cultivation of virtues. While trusting in the providence, mercy, and grace of God, Vincent was also convinced that we must cultivate our virtues in readying to perform the works of God properly. He repeated that a person who has both wisdom and humility is the treasure of a community.[14]

In a Conference of 6 December 1658, Vincent explained the purpose of the Congregation of the Mission. He emphasized that all should have freedom of heart without personal attachment to one work or another:

> Such being the case, those break the rule who do not wish to go on missions or who, having gone on them and suffered some inconvenience, do not wish to return to them, or who, taking pleasure in working in seminaries, do not wish to leave them or who, taking pleasure in some other work, are reluctant to exchange it for that of the missions, which is so necessary…. Something which will greatly help us toward this is to render ourselves indifferent to the kind of work we do.[15]

---

[14] Román, *Biography*, 284-288.

[15] *Rules, Conferences, and Writings*, 142-143.

It is clear that for Vincent the virtue of indifference is very practical, and manifests itself through one's willingness to go wherever they are sent to do the work. Vincent presents Jesus as the model, saying that the Son of God was always open to the will of the Father. However, Vincent knew that the virtue of indifference was achieved only through self-surrender and self-emptiness. When the local superior in Rome told Vincent they should compete with other congregations and sent him a detailed plan of development, Vincent wrote to him: "Please have greater confidence in God and let him steer our little ship."[16] It is interesting that he did not think acquiring this freedom of heart required much in the way of acquired knowledge or social status. For instance, Vincent encouraged the missioners to direct women to render service to God and the public in the best possible way that poor young women were capable of doing. Vincent's conclusion was concise: "In this way, both sexes served God equally."[17]

Among the 120 conferences to the Daughters of Charity we find five which include the title "Indifference." In Conference 25 (1 May 1646) Vincent delineated the disposition of inner freedom Daughters should have concerning their places of residence, their ministries, the qualities required for Sisters sent to them, and the means of carrying out their obligations well. Vincent was not afraid to state that indifference was the foundation of their life: "We'll begin with the first point, which is indifference, and so necessary to your Company that when it is no longer found in it, that will be a sure sign of its downfall."[18] In Conference 48 (14 July 1651) Vincent restated that indifference should characterize the disposition of a Daughter of Charity in going to any place, whether she be sent or called there, with any Sister, and as a means of keeping themselves from yielding to the weaknesses that could make them want to leave.[19] In Conference 73 (6 June 1656) Vincent explained the content of attachment as a disordered affection, as for some creature that is loved, not for the love of God but some other motive. He distinguished two kinds of attachment: one for what we have, the other for what we desire.[20] Then he offered a vivid image of the state of being attached: "To understand better what's meant by an attachment, dear Sisters, picture a man tied to a tree by a rope, his hands and feet bound in chains, with the rope well knotted

---

[16] Louis Abelly, *The Life of the Venerable Servant of God: Vincent de Paul*, trans. William Quinn, F.S.C., with additional annotation by Edward R. Udovic, C.M., vols. 1-3 (Vincentian Studies Institute, New City Press, 1993), 3:27.

[17] *Rules, Conference, and Writings*, 145.

[18] CCD, 9:201.

[19] Ibid., 401.

[20] Ibid., 10:129.

and the chains well riveted; what can he do? There he is enslaved."[21] In this state he cannot free himself nor look for something to sustain his life.

It is intriguing to note that these three conferences on indifference were delivered at five year intervals, as though Vincent, and probably Louise, who lived with the Daughters as their superior, felt the need to continually stress the importance of this virtue. The apostolic character of indifference is most clearly described in Conferences 116 (8 December 1659) and 117 (14 December 1659), his last two talks to the Daughters before the death of Louise de Marillac.[22] Vincent utilized the example of a mare, or carriage horse, which allows herself to be driven wherever people want:

> Isn't it a great pity that senseless animals teach us this lesson of indifference, and we have such trouble practicing it! Sisters, let's keep firmly in mind this lesson of our Lord, who submitted in all things to the Will of His Father; remember that well and ask Him fervently in your prayers for the grace of being always indifferent to all sorts of ministries, in one place or another, be they important or lowly, ready for whatever pleases Him.[23]

Quoting Psalm 73:22, "I have become like a beast of burden." Vincent insisted that Jesus himself became like a horse with no will but that of his Father. In all of his conferences and letters the primary example was always Jesus on earth who lived for the poor. Vincent clearly realized that it was indifference that frees the human heart to fulfill their vocation: "Here's what indifference is, Sister: it's a virtue that causes us not to refuse anything or to desire anything. To wish for nothing, to reject nothing, but to accept whatever God may send us through our Superiors; in a word, Sisters, an indifferent person is one who wants to do nothing but the Will of God. That's what is meant by being indifferent."[24] Here we realize Vincent was a mystic, a selfless man who taught his followers to practice kenosis in every day and every aspect of life.

Then, from whom did Vincent learn the mystic spirituality of indifference? I have mentioned that Benet of Canfield's *The Rule of Perfection*

---

[21] *Ibid.*, 132. Vincent describes three kinds of attachment: vanity, fastidiousness, and esteem.

[22] Louise de Marillac died 15 March 1660. After her death, Vincent gave his final conferences on the virtue of Louise (Conferences 118 and 119), and on the election of her successor (Conference 120). Therefore, it can be said that his final two conferences on indifference were, in fact, his last words to the Daughters of Charity.

[23] *CCD*, 10:560.

[24] *Ibid.*, 562.

greatly influenced Vincent during the initial period of his conversion. Benet of Canfield presented rules for knowing the will of God: "all things which offer themselves to be done or suffered, approved or withstood, whether corporal or spiritual, are of three kinds, namely commanded, forbidden, or indifferent. Nothing can happen which is not comprised in one of these three kinds."[25] Two things are commanded or forbidden, orders to be followed. It is the third kind, those which are indifferent, that requires true discretion. He believed that God has left the greatest part of our lives to choice, to do or to leave undone, to accept or reject without sin the indifferent. He concluded, "How can something tend toward perfection which puts aside obedience and nourishes self-will, the root of all imperfection?"[26] Although Benet of Canfield focused on this vast realm of indifferent action and freedom of choice as a field for practicing perfection, he did not develop the virtue of indifference. However, he did expound upon an important aspect in Vincent's spirituality, integrating contemplation and action: "This is the true active and contemplative life, not separated (as many take it to be), but joined together, making exterior works interior, temporal ones spiritual, and obscurities luminous, and finally, joining contemplation and action in the same work without prejudice or hindrance to either."[27]

Ultimately, it was Saint Francis de Sales, the bishop of Geneva, who became the model of sanctity for Vincent. Vincent met him in 1618 and 1619, when going through a period of purification (1617-1625), aspiring to transform his moody and melancholic character to the "perfect equilibrium" of Francis de Sales. Vincent often said "How good must God be since the Bishop of Geneva is so good." Several meetings were enough to knit a solid friendship between the two. Both longed for a profound reformation of the clergy and a simplified form of preaching.[28] Vincent learned to live in the presence of God, the virtue of detachment and indifference, humility, joy, and gentleness from Francis de Sales. Vincent's letter to Louise (Letter 49, around 1630) offers his source of indifference: "Blessed be God that you are freed from the first attachment. We shall talk about the other one when next we meet; I mean about the one for your confessor.... Read the book concerning the love of God, in particular the one that deals with God's Will

---

[25] *Renaissance Dialectic and Renaissance Piety: Benet of Canfield's "Rule of Perfection": A Translation and Study*, ed. & trans. Kent Emery, Jr. (Binghamton, New York: Medieval and Renaissance Texts and Studies, 1987), 111.

[26] *Ibid.*, 118.

[27] *Ibid.*, 119.

[28] André Dodin, C.M., *Vincent de Paul and Charity: A Contemporary Portrait of His Life and Apostolic Spirit*, trans. Jean Marie Smith and Dennis Saunders (New City Press, 1993), 26.

and indifference…. God is love and wants us to go to Him through love."[29] It is clear that for Vincent the virtue of indifference is a pure disposition of heart, free from all the attachments which hinder us from perfect love. In reading the conferences, as his understanding of apostolic spirituality further deepened, his understanding of the virtue of indifference became more practical and concrete. The fruit of indifference is the freedom of heart manifested in every aspect of our life.

Statue of Zhu Xi, White Deer Grotto Academy, Jiujiang, Jiangxi province, China.
Public Domain

2. Absence of Private Mind in Cheng Yi

Reflections on Things at Hand (近思錄), edited by Zhu Xi/Chu Hsi and Lü Tsu-Ch'ien in 1175, is a Neo-Confucian anthology of the four most

---

[29] *CCD*, 1:80-1. Francis de Sales talks about the loving, pure, or holy indifference in his *Treatise on the Love of God*, Book 9, chapters 4-9.

famous Confucian scholars of the Northern Song period. They initiated a new trend of Confucianism and the book became a standard introductory text for generations. Among the 622 articles compiled in this anthology half are regarded as the words of Cheng Yi, the philosophical mentor of Zhu Xi. He insisted that Confucian learning should be a guide toward becoming a sage, wanting to distinguish it from the prevalent Buddhism. Cheng Yi stated that a Confucian should not talk about the absence of mind (無心), but rather the absence of private / selfish mind (無私心): "Someone advocated the doctrine of the absence of mind. I-ch'uan (pen name of Cheng Yi) said, 'The absence of mind is wrong. We should say only the absence of a selfish mind.'"[30] The absence of mind is a Zen Buddhist way of cultivation which negates any permanent principle, or norm of good and evil, in itself. Cheng Yi wished to make clear that the principle of Heaven (天理) is innate in the human heart / mind, and one must get rid of the private mind which seeks disordered personal benefit. In Confucian tradition, wherein socio-political concerns are the ultimate good, the public, or impartiality (公), stood for the principle of Heaven, while the private (私) represented selfish desires that divert a person from realizing what is right.

Therefore, in Neo-Confucianism impartiality is esteemed as the chief character of benevolence (*jen / ren* 仁, also translated as humanity), the perfection of all virtues:

> "Essentially speaking, the way of humanity may be expressed in one word, namely, impartiality. However, impartiality is but the principle of humanity; it should not be equated with humanity itself. When one makes impartiality the substance of his person, that is humanity. Because of his impartiality, there will be no distinction between himself and others. Therefore a man of humanity is a man of both altruism and love. Altruism is the application of humanity, while love is its function."[31]

Then what constitutes the "private mind?" Cheng Yi believed it to be not only when a person's intention is oriented toward private concerns, but when it is out of proportion with the balance of one's original nature (本然之性):

---

[30] *Reflections on Things at Hand: The Neo-Confucian Anthology*, compiled by Chu Hsi and Lü Tsu-ch'ien, trans. with notes by Wing-Tsit Chan (Columbia University Press, 1967), 71 (II-76).

[31] *Ibid.*, 62 (II-52).

When one is activated by Heaven, he will be free from error, but when he is activated by human desires (人欲), he will err. Great is the meaning of the hexagram, *wu-wang* (無妄, absence of falsehood). Even if one has no perverse mind, if he is not in accord with the correct principle (正理), he will err, and that amounts to having a perverse mind (邪心). If one is free from error, he will not go away from the correct principle, for to go away means to err.[32]

In his commentary on Hexagram 25, Cheng Yi compares *wu-wang-zhe* (無妄者), or absence of falsehood, with *wang-zhe* (妄者), falsehood. He explains that a person who follows the principle with utmost sincerity is free from falsehood and united with the life-giving power of Heaven and Earth. Everything in the natural world is without falsehood, so that in watching images of nature the sage nurtures all things according to their proper place and time. But when the human heart follows its own desire and falls into excess, one falls into falsehood.[33] What rises above the mean (中) is wrong and private. In his commentary on Hexagram 13, *Tongren* (同人), or Fellowship, Cheng Yi states that sages possess a heart of great impartiality (大公之心) and public appeal, while ordinary people appeal to those with private considerations (私意) benefitting only a few. It is when a leader fulfills the principle of Heaven that a community of great unity (大同之體) is formed, and its fragrance spreads far and wide.

Cheng Yi offers concrete examples of how we can overcome our private mind. First, he advises us to learn to share what we have with others. In his commentary on the Fifth Yang line of Hexagram 9, *Xiaoxu* (小畜), or Lesser Domestication, he writes: "The Fifth Yang means to help and deliver each other, as the rich assisting their neighbors. The Fifth Yang is the position of the prince, and so it is like the wealthy man who shares his riches." Sharing our riches is the beginning, something which moves the hearts of people. Then, we must go further and learn to listen to others. In his commentary on the Fifth Yang line of Hexagram 19, *Lin* (臨), or Overseeing, Cheng Yi focuses on the importance of listening: "If one trusts their knowledge, they will not become wise. Only if one is able to gather the good people of the whole world and entrust to them the works of the world, every concern will be taken care of. When one does not trust one's

---

[32] *Ibid.*, 44 (II-8). Confucian scholars generally agree that this entire passage is Cheng Yi's interpretation of Hexagram 25.

[33] Hexagram 25; Commentary on Top Yang (過於理則妄也).

own wisdom, then their wisdom will become great."[34] When we overcome our attachment to our own ideas, we are not only freed from our private mind but we open to all other ideas for the benefit of the whole. In other words, freeing oneself from one's private mind possesses a social or apostolic character in itself.

Cheng Yi utilizes an image of a mountain, depicted with fire at its base, as a perfect model for our effort to overcome the private mind in Hexagram 22, *Bi* (賁), or Elegance. He states, "The mountain is a place where plants and hundreds of things live together. At its bottom a fire burns, beautifully adorning the mountain in its brilliant light. The noble person, looking at the mountain and the light of the fire, makes an effort to order political affairs brightly. He accomplishes cultural governance, but dares not pass fast judgment on legal issues. In making judgments on legal matters, rulers must be careful and prudent."[35] Cheng Yi also mentions the serious nature of legal affairs in Hexagrams 21 and 6, wherein he asserts that to settle legal suits impartially, without being too harsh or too weak, one has to hold to the Middle Path (中道) without private mind.

It would be ideal to govern the state so as not to face legal problems, but a leader must be ready to tackle the rough and dirty problems of a nation in order to rectify corruption. Therefore, a leader has to learn "the constant principle of stretching and shrinking, coming and going."[36] Generosity, moreover, has to be practiced properly. Knowing the right time to act is the highest wisdom in Confucian tradition, and this involves discernment (Hexagrams 17, 30, 64). In the end it is only through cultivating such virtue that we learn to overcome our private mind and falsehood (Hexagram 29).

Cheng Yi presented three stages of self-cultivation:[37] first is receiving the norms of propriety which frees us from bad habits and unworthy values; second is transforming our temperament by overcoming disordered desires; and third is striving to reach a state of mind empty and free from selfishness (虛中無我). When we maintain this state of mind, we are capable of responding to every event with the Timely Mean (時中). Since Cheng Yi and other Neo-Confucian scholars demanded constant human effort, and

---

[34] 故自任其知者，適足爲不知，唯能取天下之善，任天下之總明，則无所不周，是不自任其知，則其知大矣。These English translations of Cheng Yi's commentaries on the *Book of Changes* are mine.

[35] Cheng Yi's commentary on the image of the mountain (山者草木百物之所聚生也，火在其下而上照庶類，皆被其光明，爲賁飾之象也。君子觀山下有火明照之象，以修明其庶政，成文明之治，而无果敢於折獄也。折獄者，人君之所致愼也).

[36] Hexagram 11, Tai 泰 Peace, Cheng Yi's commentary on the images of the Third Yang (屈伸往來之常理也).

[37] *Reflections on Things at Hand*, 45-50 (II-9, 10, and 21).

encouraged us to transform our temperament, we might presume they taught that we can attain an absence of private desires with will-power. However, they warned that in this stage of self-cultivation we must be passive: "People say we must practice with effort. Such a statement, however, is superficial. If a person really knows that a thing should be done, when he sees anything that should be done, he does not need to wait for his will to be aroused. As soon as he artificially arouses his will, that means selfishness / private mind (私心). How can such a spirit last long?"[38]

From Confucius on, Confucians knew that if we really know something we love it and find happiness in it, so that things come naturally without arousing self-will (which can easily become selfish pride). It is noteworthy that even though Confucians have no notion of grace, the authentic state-of-mind unified with the principle of Heaven is to be achieved without self-will. Cheng Yi praised humility and gentleness as the most important human virtue. In his commentary on Hexagram 14, *Dayou* (大有), or Great Holdings, and 15, *Qian* (謙), or Modesty, Cheng Yi states that humility is the utmost virtue – a humble person always attains the mean and never surpasses the norm. If leaders maintain gentleness, the hearts of the people return to them.

Line drawing of Cheng Yi (1033-1107).
Public Domain

---

[38] *Ibid.*, 63 (II-54).

Finally, in his commentary on Hexagram 27, *Yi* (頤), or nourishment, Cheng Yi describes the fruit of emptying the private mind. Here again Cheng Yi adopts the symbol of the mountain, which provides life and nourishment: "The image of this Hexagram depicts a mountain at top, thunder at its base. As the bottom of the mountain shakes, all the roots of the trees vibrate and the buds of life emerge. In a word, it is the image of nurturing…. Looking at this image, the noble person cultivates themselves: by being prudent in what they say, they nurture virtue; by being moderate in what they eat, they nurture the body."[39] And, in beginning his commentary, Cheng Yi encompasses the four areas of human need within the context of nourishment (頤養之道): the nourishing of life (養生); nourishing of body (養形); nourishing of virtue (養德); and nourishing of people (養人). When we cultivate ourselves in overcoming our private mind, we gradually attain a freedom of heart that enables us to nurture the human world (萬民), and also understand how heaven and earth nurture the natural world (萬物). Cheng Yi's absence of private mind, therefore, can be seen to resemble Vincent de Paul's indifference in their social and apostolic influence.

3. The Daoist Interpretation of the Ordinary Mind (平常心) in Yin Zhiping

The term "Ordinary Mind" is used in all three traditional religions of China, Confucianism, Buddhism, and Daoism, with a common emphasis on daily, mundane life.[40] Yet the distinctive colors and nuances within each tradition make it important to perceive its unique meaning. In Neo-Confucianism it is the moral mind cultivated in ordinary political life (social responsibility in the family, local community, nation, and international world), overcoming one's private desires and thereby achieving an all encompassing virtue of benevolence. In Zen Buddhism it is the enlightened mind performing ordinary daily activity (walking, eating, sitting, and sleeping), eliminating attachments which cause suffering and anxiety. In the Complete Perfection School of Daoism it is the mind of equilibrium (emptied of private inclinations and evil thought), responding properly to worldly change.

---

[39] Hexagram 27, Cheng Yi's commentary on the image of the mountain (以二體言之山下有雷, 雷震於山下山之生物皆動其根荄, 發其萌芽爲養之象。…故君子觀其象, 以養其身, 愼言語以養其德, 節飲食以養其體).

[40] Gu Jae-hye 具載會, "Studies on the Theory of Cultivation by the Longmen Branch of Complete Reality" (전진교 용문파 수행론에 대한 연구) [master's thesis, Sogang University, 1997], 57. As an appendix to his thesis, he translated the complete text of Yin Zhiping's conferences into Korean, pp. 84-168.

Yin Zhiping attempted to integrate the three religions with his use of the term "Ordinary Mind":

> Since worldly people did not attain "Ordinary Constancy (平常者)" and have no controller for their heart/mind, their feeling chases after things of fashion and their life energy is wasted in various holes of their body. Mencius stated that the purposeful will (志) should be the master of life energy (氣). When a person is capable of governing life energy with a purposeful will and letting it not be wasted, the life energy transforms itself into the bright light, and when it is accumulated, it becomes the Great Brilliant Light. My teacher Changchuan used to say that the Great Brilliant Light wraps the purple golden lotus which signifies our heart. In order to let the brilliant spiritual energy stay within our heart, we have to first attain ordinary constancy, and after that we can reach this state of light. Confucius talked about the Middle Path (中道), by which he also meant ordinary constancy. And there is a Buddhist saying that Buddha nature originally has no enlightenment and all sentient beings are not dismayed. The mind people ordinarily use is the enlightened mind. If we do not know constancy, there will be disorder and disaster, while we know constancy (常), there will be brightness (明).[41]

A portrait of Confucius (551-479 BC).
Public Domain

---

[41] *The Records of the Northern Journey*, 26:727, third section. 世人所以不得平常者, 爲心無主宰, 情逐物流, 其氣耗散於衆竅之中. <<孟子>> 之說爲志, 云志者氣之帥也. 人能以志帥氣, 不令耗散, 則化成光明, 積之成大光明. 師父有云. 大光明罩紫金蓮. 蓮喩心也, 神明處焉, 必先平常而後能致此. 孔子說中道, 亦平常之義. 又有云. 佛性元無悟, 衆生本不迷, 平常用心處, 即此是菩提. 不知常, 妄作凶, 知常則明.

This very clearly states how Yin Zhiping conceived the concept of Ordinary Mind. There are two layers of meaning: one denotes daily ordinariness, which all three religions take seriously; the other denotes knowing constancy, which is the Dao, the unchangeable way embedded in ordinary affairs. Even though he accepts the priority of moral will over life energy, as suggested by Mencius, and identifies the Confucian Middle Path with Ordinary Constancy, he cites the uniquely Daoistic dual cultivation of mind and energy. And although he quotes a Zen Buddhist saying on Ordinary Mind, he interprets it with *Daodejing*, chapter 16, which teaches knowing constant Dao will lead to immortality.

As the sixth patriarch of the Complete Perfection Order (1228-1238), and during the most prosperous period under early Mongol reign, Yin Zhiping 尹志平 took a long journey through the Northeastern part of China giving evening lectures to Daoist masters and lay people. In his words we grasp what he meant by the Ordinary Mind, how one achieved a state of ordinary constancy, and what was the effect of attaining it.

First, what did he mean by Ordinary Mind? Yin Zhiping describes our mind as the bright moon (心月) which shines on everything, so long as it is not obscured by private feeling (私情) and wrong thought (邪念) which float like clouds.[42] If we clear away our private thoughts and feelings, our mind can shine on every event as brightly as the moon in the sky. Therefore, we have to cultivate our mind in order to reach ordinary constancy: "The Dao originally does not act, therefore we have to realize our mind. If we govern our mind (治其心) and attain the state of ordinary constancy, the Dao will come to life by itself…. Even though the Seven Perfected Ones received the teaching from their Master Wang Zhe, they controlled their minds (制其心) hundreds and thousands of times."[43] He also states that through the mind of equanimity (平心) we transform our body and life energy and return to our heaven endowed nature.

Then, what is the effect of attaining the state of ordinary constancy? Yin Zhiping explains three stages of the Daoist transformation: when our heart/mind is balanced and constant, our spiritual energy (神) is settled and calm; when our spiritual energy is calm, vital energy (精) is congealed; and when vital energy is congealed, all life energy (氣) is harmonized. This harmonious calmness is reflected transparently on our face and discernible

---

[42] *Ibid.*, 734, third section. 又提月曰, 此物但不爲青霄之下, 浮雲障蔽, 則虛明洞蔽, 無物不照, 人皆見之。 見殊不知, 人人有此心月, 但爲浮雲所蔽, 則失其明, 凡私情邪念即浮雲也。 人能常使邪念不生, 則心月如天月之明, 與天地相終始, 而不復昧矣。

[43] *Ibid.*, 737, third section. 道本無爲, 惟其了心而已… 豈不見諸師眞, 親授教於祖師, 然猶千磨百鍊, 以制其心.

in our four limbs.[44] It is crucial to observe that every level of our life energy is purified and transformed through our daily actions. Yin Zhiping describes this world as his retreat "hut" (環堵: a tiny room with walls), where he can wander and mingle with everything while enjoying freedom of heart.[45] A person who has attained the constant ordinary mind can freely choose non-action or action. "The ordinary constancy is the true constancy. The heart/mind responds to all kinds of changes, but is not affected by outside things; it always responds, but it is always quiet. Gradually it enters the true Dao. The ordinary constancy is the Dao."[46] Therefore, Yin Zhiping confidently concludes that only the Ordinary Mind can last long, and that purity of heart is not evident only through inner cultivation but through external activities, i.e., both in non-action and action. In other words, the Ordinary Mind leads a person to become an apostolic mystic who keeps their heart bright as the moon in the midst of the ever-changing events of life.

Conclusion

We have discussed the virtue of indifference in Vincent de Paul, the absence of the private mind in Cheng Yi, and the state of Ordinary Mind in Yin Zhiping. Their commonality resides in reaching the state of a human heart freed from selfish desires, attachment to personal plans and benefit, and from self-image. This freedom of heart leaves a person totally open, imbued with a "passionate passivity" that enables complete commitment to apostolic mission or sage governance. I call this the fruit of apostolic mysticism and argue this to be the only verifiable proof that one's mystical spirituality is authentic and healthy.

That said, we must admit that according to whom their conferences were directed there is a definite cultural difference among the three mystics. Vincent de Paul was talking to his companies of religious men and women to be sent about the world in service of the poor. Their virtue of indifference was to be made manifest through their acts of obedience. He knew very well that this kind of obedience would not last long unless rooted in the love of God, and in the spiritual maturity which comes from an inner freedom of heart. Cheng Yi was talking to Confucian students and intellectuals who were either government officials or preparing to be. Therefore the absence of the private mind bears a strong political tone, examples being the use of one's riches for neighbors, listening to people's opinions, and the

---

[44] *Ibid.*, 736, third section.

[45] *Ibid.*, 734, second section.

[46] *Ibid.*, 727, second section. 平常即眞常也. 心應萬變, 不爲物遷, 常應常靜, 漸入眞道, 平常是道也.

handling of lawsuits impartially. The cultivation of humility, gentleness, and generosity was connected with the practice of the Timely Mean in knowing the appropriate time to take proper action. Yin Zhiping was talking to Daoist masters and the lay leadership of his order, wherein the Ordinary Mind was presented as the foundation through which to integrate inner and outer cultivation, purification of mind and life energy. That we must keep a constant mind despite the feelings of happiness, anger, sadness, and joy is something shared by all three apostolic mystics.

The conflict between human attachment and the will of God in Vincent, between the private mind and the principle of Heaven in Cheng Yi, and between the Dao as a shining moon in the heart and private feelings as clouds in Yin Zhiping, creates an overarching theme. As Evelyn Underhill writes, this experience of opposition and inner conflict requires a long process of purification:

> We will begin, then, with the central fact of the mystic's experience. This central fact, it seems to me, is an overwhelming consciousness of God and of his own soul: a consciousness which absorbs or eclipses all other centers of interest.... Reviewing the firsthand declarations of the mystics, we inevitably notice one prominent feature: the frequency with which they break up their experience into three phases.... Sometimes they regard them subjectively, and speak of three stages of growth through which they pass, such as those of Beginner, Proficient, and Perfect....[47]

We identify Underhill's observations in our three mystics as well. Moreover, she affirms my contention that apostolic fruit verifies the authenticity of the mystics' spirituality. A genuine sublimation of consciousness, i.e., the mystic way, is the proportion of life itself. "'What fruit doest thou bring back from this thy vision?' is the final question which Jacopone da Todi addresses to the mystic's soul. And the answer is: 'An ordered life in every state.'"[48] I would add that an ordered life comes from indifference, the freedom of heart. Yin Zhiping also teaches us that Ordinary Mind can respond to change while remaining quiet, therefore only those who achieve ordinary constancy last. Steven Katz is partially correct in insisting

---

[47] Evelyn Underhill, "The Essentials of Mysticism," in *Understanding Mysticism*, ed. Richard Woods (New York: Doubleday, 1980), 27, 30.

[48] *Ibid.*, 41.

that mysticism is deeply tied to its root tradition, world view, and language,[49] but we cannot deny the fact that its result shares characteristics as seen in three mystics from three very different traditions.

Finally, notice that all three mystics employed central symbols from the natural world. Vincent de Paul used a mare which pulls a cart following the will of her master; Cheng Yi chose the mountain, nurturing all forms of life according to a proper time; and Yin Zhiping envisioned a bright moon which shines upon the world, though occasionally darkened by fleeting clouds. They probably chose natural examples due to their innate lack of artificiality or falsity. Cheng Yi warned as superficial the notion of practice with effort, believing that as we artificially arouse our will it becomes selfishness. Yin Zhiping asserted that preserving a constant mind and accumulating worldly merits derives from the person, but the manifestation of the Dao, and the sages leading you, belong to Heaven.[50] Paradoxically, it is in this entrusting passivity that the most energetic passion for apostolic outreach is born and preserved.

---

[49] Steven T. Katz, "The Conservative Character of Mystical Experience," *Mysticism and Religious Traditions* (1983), 3-60.

[50] *The Records of the Northern Journey*, 736, second section. 先保此平常, 其積行累功, 皆由乎己, 是在我者也. 道之顯驗, 聖賢把握, 是在天者也. 當盡其在我者, 而任其在天者, 功行既至, 道乃自得.

A Challenge to Napoleon: The Defiance of the Daughters of Charity
By
Elisabeth Charpy, D.C.
Translated by
Clara Orban, Ph.D.
&
Edward R. Udovic, C.M.

"In the presence of God and of the Heavenly Host, for a year I renew my baptismal promises and make a vow to God of poverty, chastity and obedience, in accordance with our rule and our statutes. I also vow to work towards corporeal and spiritual service to the sick poor, our true masters, in the Company of the Daughters of Charity. I ask this by the merits of Jesus Christ crucified and through the intercession of the very holy Virgin."

In France, the coup d'état of 18 Brumaire (9 November 1799) brought Napoleon Bonaparte to power. The Consulate gave a new breath of life to the country after the terrible years of the Revolution. Bonaparte began the national reconstruction by reestablishing civil peace. Most of the émigrés were authorized to return. The population rallied behind the new master of France.

Restoration of the Daughters of Charity — 22 December 1800

The re-establishment of the Daughters was spurred, in part, by hospital directors, who were worried about the decline of care in their establishments, and who wanted the former sisters to resume their services. In 1800 Sister Thérèse Deschaux, superior of the Hospital at Auch, was sent to Paris, to meet with the Minister of Cults, Jean-Antoine Chaptal.[1]

---

[1] Born 1756 in Saint-Pierre-de-Nogaret, Lozère, Chaptal studied chemistry at the University of Montpellier, where he earned his doctorate in 1777 and later became a professor. A factory he established was the first to commercially produce sulfuric acid in France, and his scientific accomplishments led to recognition and awards from the French government. Chaptal was arrested and briefly imprisoned during the French Revolution for publishing a controversial paper. Following his release he managed the saltpetre works at Grenelle. He was appointed councilor of state by the First Consul after the 18 Brumaire coup of 9 November 1799, and eventually Minister of the Interior. As such, he instituted many reforms in the fields of medicine, industry, and public works — including a reorganization of the hospitals and the introduction of the metric system. Chaptal fell in and out of favor with Napoleon, who awarded him the Grand Cross of the Legion of Honor less than a year after forcing him from office in 1804. He concluded his career as director-general of commerce and manufacturing and Minister of State, before the Bourbon Restoration forced him to permanently retire. He died in Paris in 1832.

He acknowledged the deplorable state of the hospitals: "I am tired of the innumerable complaints that arrive daily and the unsatisfactory state of hospices."

Having learned that the superioress general of the Daughters of Charity had returned to Paris, he expressed his desire to re-establish their Company, dismantled in 1792 along with other secular religious congregations.

On 22 December 1800, having become Minister of the Interior, Chaptal published a decree which brought the Company of the Daughters of Charity back to life:

> Art. 1. Citizen Deleau, formerly the superior of the Daughters of Charity, is authorized to prepare students to serve in hospices.
> Art. 2. The orphanage located on the Rue du Vieux Colombier, is put at their disposal.
> Art. 7. The necessary funds to support the needs of the institution will be taken from the general funds budgeted for hospices. This will not exceed the sum of twelve thousand francs.[2]

Antoinette Deleau, D.C.
Superioress General, 1790-1804.
Archives, Daughters of Charity, Paris

On 25 January 1801, Mother Antoinette Deleau moved into the Rue du Vieux Colombier with some of the sisters who had returned to Paris. Soon, postulants arrived from all regions of France. Sixty-five were welcomed

---

[2] Chevalier A., *Les Sœurs de la Charité et le conseil municipal de Paris* (1881).

during the year. A new decree, dated 19 April, permitted the Daughters of Charity to resume their ministries in the various arrondissements of Paris under the supervision of local committees established by the government:

> Art. 5. Subject to inspection by the committees, the Daughters of Charity are especially charged with the assistance and comfort of the sick poor of each arrondissement, and the assistance of children of a young age and with the distribution of linen, beds, clothes, furniture and other things which, by usage and propriety only they can direct.
> Art. 6. There are in each municipal arrondissement soup kitchens for the poor and warehouses for medicines. Their direction is conferred to the Daughters of Charity.[3]

In her circular letter of 1 January 1802, Mother Antoinette Deleau expressed her joy at the Company's restoration:

> Here we are, restored by the French Government to that identity which we never stopped being according to our joyous vocation: the humble servants of the poor... I know of the virtuous actions that distinguished many of you during all the trials of the Revolution....[4] Let us make a generous resolution to renew ourselves in the love and the exercise of all our duties. The renovation of our vows which usually takes place on 25 March[5] should take place immediately upon reception of the present letter.[6]

---

[3] *Ibid.*

[4] During the Revolution, sisters were imprisoned, where some died, and some were even executed in Arras, Angers, and Cambrai. For instance, at Arras (Robespierre's birthplace, and therefore a town fiercely loyal to the Revolution's ideals), the superioress, Marie-Madeleine Fontaine, along with three sisters, Marie-Françoise Lanel, Thérèse-Madeleine Fantou, and Jeanne Gérard, were jailed 14 February 1794 for refusing to take the government's newly prescribed oaths. Eventually they were charged with possession of counter-revolutionary printed matter (evidence exists that it was planted) and imprisoned. It was soon determined that their good charitable works would make it difficult, even in Arras, to have them executed. Subsequently they were moved to Cambrai where, on 26 June 1794, they were guillotined. It is said that as their sentence was issued, and at their execution, the normally boisterous crowd remained silent.

[5] The vows of the Daughters of Charity are renewed annually on the Feast of the Annunciation, 25 March, with the permission of the superior general of the Congregation of the Mission.

[6] Archives, Daughters of Charity, Maison-Mère, 140, rue du Bac, Paris, France. Hereinafter cited as D.C. Archives.

The Company of the Daughters of Charity, like the rest of the Church in France, began to reorganize itself. Many houses (hospitals, houses of Charity) were established. Postulants continued to arrive in great numbers: eighty-three in 1802, seventy-six in 1803. The sisters resumed the annual renewal of their vows.

On 8 April 1802, the Chamber of Deputies ratified the concordat with the Holy See, signed the preceding 15 July.[7] In addition, it recognized the seventy-seven Gallican "organic articles" which Bonaparte had unilaterally added to the agreement. For example, pontifical decrees could not be published without governmental approval. Nonetheless, the French welcomed with relief the renewal of religious life. With the news that pastors would be required to swear an oath of fidelity the sisters became worried. Would the imposition of this oath lead again to the strife caused by the oath during the Revolution?[8] On 4 June 1802, Jean-Étienne-Marie Portalis, the Minister of Cults, responded to the prefect of the Seine's questions in this regard:

> The Daughters of Charity wonder whether they will be required to take the same oaths required of those who are employed as pastors or others involved in ministry to souls. All these ecclesiastics are required to do when they swear the oath required by the Concordat is to promise to live in communion with the bishops nominated by the first Consul and confirmed by the Pope.

---

[7] The Concordat of 1801 was an agreement between Napoleon Bonaparte and Pope Pius VII that solidified the Roman Catholic Church as the majority church of France and brought back most of its civil statutes. However, while the Concordat restored some ties to the papacy, it largely favored the state. Napoleon believed he could win favor with French Catholics while also controlling Rome's political reach.

[8] Passed on 12 July 1790, the Civil Constitution of the Clergy was a law which effectively made the Roman Catholic Church subordinate to the French government. In the year leading to its passing, the State had already eradicated tithing, nationalized Church property utilized to create revenue, forbade the taking of monastic vows, and dissolved all ecclesiastical orders and congregations beyond those involved in nursing or the education of children. The new law further reduced Rome's authority in: significantly reducing the number of bishops; mandating that bishops and priests be elected locally only by those who had sworn an oath to the government (and that those who voted did not need to be Catholic); reducing the Pope's role in appointing clergy to only being allowed the right of being informed of election results; and demanding that new bishops swear an oath of loyalty to the State before taking office. Furthermore, on 27 November 1790, the National Assembly directed the clergy to sign an oath of loyalty to the Constitution. Many refused the oath, which led to great internal discord. Religious freedoms were restored in 1795, but it was not until the Concordat of 1801 that the civilly constituted Gallican Church resolved this conflict with Rome.

It is foreseen and it is the intention of the government that the Daughters of Charity recognize as their superior the diocesan bishop. It is enough to accept their declaration of intent to obey their bishop without burdening them with other obligations which are foreign to their sex and to the nature of their work.[9]

On 22 August sixty sisters gathered in an Assembly presided over by their director, Laurent Philippe. The term of the superioress general, Mother Deleau, despite her age (seventy-five years old, fifty-five of vocation), was extended and Sister Thérèse Deschaux (fifty-nine years old, thirty-nine of vocation), superior of the Hospital at Auch, was named assistant.

A new decree, signed on 16 October 1802 by Napoleon clarified the rules concerning the Company of the Daughters of Charity:

> Art. 1. As in the past, the sisters, called of Charity, are authorized to consecrate themselves to the service of the sick in hospices and parishes and to the instruction of poor girls.
> Art. 2. They can wear their traditional costume.
> Art. 3. They are in a religious order under the jurisdiction of the bishops; they will not correspond with any foreign superior.
> Art. 5. They may only receive new recruits in their Paris house.[10]

At the time it does not seem that the article placing the Company of the Daughters of Charity under the jurisdiction of the local bishop posed any problem. In 1802, the Congregation of the Mission had not yet been legally reestablished in France.

During the seventeenth century, Louise de Marillac, co-founder of the Daughters of Charity with Vincent de Paul, had insisted that the community should depend on the superior general of the Congregation of the Mission rather than the bishops. At the time there was still some opposition among the bishops to having consecrated women not under the rule of cloister. For Louise and Vincent, enclosing the Daughters of Charity in their houses would lead to the end of their direct service to the poor, thereby countering the very goal of their Company. Assuring the juridical link between the Congregation

---

[9] Chevalier A., *Les Sœurs de la Charité*.

[10] Chevalier, A., *Les Soeurs de la Charité*; and Archives Nationales, Paris, France: F/19/6344 (Hereinafter cited as AN).

of the Mission and the Company of the Daughters of Charity was, for Louise de Marillac, not only a matter of protecting the Daughters' ministry to the poor, but also ensuring that they would share a common spirituality.

In her circular letter of 1 January 1803, Mother Deleau announced the provisions of the decree signed by the first Consul on 16 October: She said "We are certain of the provisions of this decree but we have not yet received a copy of it."[11]

Many requests for sisters came to Mother Deleau from all over the country. Despite their growing numbers, Mother Deleau could not fulfill all the requests. For example, she responded to the municipality of Châtillon-sur-Seine: "We receive many requests of this type which, due to lack of personnel, we cannot satisfy… We would need 3,000 sisters to fill the demand, and there is only at best half that number."[12]

On 30 January 1804, Sister Deschaux, announced the death of Mother Antoinette Deleau the night of the 29th, around midnight. The sisters, for their part, appreciated the courage and wisdom Mother Deleau had exercised in leading the Daughters of Charity during the years of the Revolution. They acknowledged her role as the restorer of the Company.

On the Monday after Pentecost, 21 May 1804, according to the Company's custom the sisters gathered in Paris for the election of their next superioress general. They chose Sister Thérèse Deschaux (sixty-one years old, forty-one of vocation). The superior of the Petites-Maisons de Paris, Sister Marie Quitterie Duprat (fifty-eight years old, forty-one of vocation), was elected to replace her in the office of assistant.

Several days later on 27 May, an imperial decree reestablished the Congregation of the Mission under the name *Society of Priests Charged with Preparing and Furnishing Missionaries to Serve French Missions in the Levant and China*. The director of this society would be named by the Emperor.[13]

Napoleon's control of the Congregations — 1804-1805

The Concordat had given Napoleon all but complete control over the episcopacy. He also wanted to establish his authority over religious communities. From his perspective their existence was justified by their social utility. After his coronation by Pope Pius VII, as Emperor of the French, he set out to re-establish a close alliance between Church and State.

---

[11] D.C. Archives.

[12] D.C. Archives.

[13] Archives, Congregation of the Mission, Maison-Mère, 95, rue de Sevres, Paris, France. Hereinafter cited as C.M. Archives.

Beginning in 1804, Napoleon published a number of decrees concerning religious congregations. The decree of 22 June 1804, for example, obliged any association or religious congregation which wished to operate in France to obtain legal authorization from the Emperor. This same decree directed all congregations who had already been legally recognized (this included the Company of the Daughters of Charity) "to present within six months a copy of their statutes and rules so that these could be reviewed and approved by the *Conseil d'Etat* which had responsibility over all religious matters."[14]

In response to this Napoleonic decree the Pope was asked to confirm the juridical ties between the Priests of the Mission and the Daughters of Charity. A pontifical brief was issued on 30 October 1804 which stated: "To the office of the superior general of the Mission is joined the care and the government of the community of women or Daughters of Charity."[15] The six month period for compliance foreseen by the decree of 24 June was extended several times.

On 23 March 1805, Napoleon named his mother, Laetitia Bonaparte, the protector of all the so-called Sisters of Charity established throughout the Empire.[16] Madame Mère, as the Emperor's mother was called, convoked a general chapter of all twenty-five of the congregations which the government considered to be the "Sisters of Charity."

Origin of the Conflict — 1807

Mother Thérèse Deschaux, her assistant Sœur Marguerite Ithier, and their secretaries spent some time reflecting on the text of the statutes which they were required to submit to the government.

The vicar general of the Lazarists, Claude-Joseph Placiard, had died on 16 September 1807. Taking advantage of this vacancy, on 28 October, Mother Deschaux sent the required copy of the statutes to the Minister of Cults. The first article of the submitted rule stated:

> The Sisters of Charity, do not form a religious order but a congregation of women devoted to the care of the sick and the instruction of the poor. They are responsible to an ecclesiastical superior whom they choose with the approval of the Archbishop of Paris, and by a superioress general and council of several sisters, who are elected every three years.[17]

---

[14] AN: F/19/6310.

[15] C.M. Archives.

[16] AN: F/19/6247.

[17] AN: F/19/6344 and 6240.

Dominique-François Hanon, C.M.
Vicar General, 1807-1816.
Image Collection of the Vincentian Studies Institute

    The reference to having an ecclesiastical superior was not omitted, but the sisters hoped to obtain the power to choose the priest themselves! Perhaps they wanted this power so that they could choose a Priest of the Mission?

    On 14 October 1807, Pius VII named Dominique Hanon (aged 50, 35 years of vocation) as vicar general of the Congregation of the Mission to replace Monsieur Placiard. He accorded him the ordinary and extraordinary powers of the superior general that had been mentioned in the brief of 30 October 1804.[18] Napoleon accepted this nomination on the 8th of January.

    When Hanon read the statutes the sisters had presented to the government, his reaction was swift. He insisted that the juridical ties between the Congregation of the Mission and the Daughters of Charity had been in existence from the very beginning of the community's history. Having been confirmed in his position by the Pope, he resubmitted the statutes with a note indicating: "In fulfillment of the designation made by Saint Vincent himself, it is the superior general of the Congregation of the Mission who is, in perpetuity, the superior general of the Daughters of Charity, and it is he who has always been chosen."[19]

    Hanon argued that any change in the government of the Company would "destroy from its foundation the constitutions, rules, vows, and distinctive spirit of their vocation which has been responsible for making them capable of rendering such important services to our homeland and indeed to all of humanity." He predicted that any change would lead to the departure of numerous sisters.

---

[18] See note 15.

[19] AN: F/19/6344 and F/19/6240.

The minister, surprised by the claims of Monsieur Hanon and the sisters, ordered research done on the history of the Company of the Daughters of Charity. The act of approval of 1655, signed by Cardinal de Retz, archbishop of Paris, was studied at length:

> [...] the Confraternity or Society will be and will remain in perpetuity under our authority and dependence and those of our successors, the Archbishops of Paris, in the exact observance of the Statutes and Regulations specified hereinafter, which we have once again approved, and do approve, by these present letters.
>
> And since God has blessed the efforts our dearly beloved Vincent de Paul has made for the success of this pious intention, we have entrusted and confided to him and by these present letters do entrust and confide to him for life the leadership and direction of the Society and Confraternity and, after him, to his successors as Superiors General of the Congregation of the Mission.[20]

This text can be compared to the first article as it appeared in 1718 in the text published by Jean Bonnet, the then superior general of the Congregation of the Mission:

> The Company of the Daughters of Charity is instituted for the honor and service of our Lord Jesus Christ in the person of the poor, particularly the sick, by assisting them in body and spirit in the manner prescribed by their rules. They are not a religious order but a community of women who work for Christian perfection and obey, according to their institution, our lords the bishops and the superior general of the Congregation of the Mission, as superior of the Company, and to the one elected their superior, as also to the officers of the community and the individual establishments.[21]

The text which was submitted to the Minister of Cults demonstrated that the approval of 1655 placed the Daughters of Charity under the

---

[20] Approval of the Company of the Daughters of Charity by Cardinal de Retz, 18 January 1655, in Pierre Coste, C.M., ed., *Vincent de Paul: Correspondence, Conferences, Documents*, ed. and trans. by Jacqueline Kilar, D.C., Marie Poole, D.C., *et al*, 1-11, 13a & 13b (New York: New City Press, 1990-2008), 13b:146. Hereinafter cited as *CCD*.

[21] Statutes of the Daughters of Charity, 1718, D.C. Archives.

dependence of the archbishop of Paris, but confided their direction to the Congregation of the Mission, and that the statutes issued by Monsieur Bonnet confirmed that the superior general of the Congregation of the Mission also served as their superior general. The conflict that now emerged centered around whether the Daughters of Charity would be dependent on the bishops, or retain their dependence on the superior general of the Congregation of the Mission.

The conflict also illustrated the rising importance of the Company of the Daughters of Charity. In 1807, only six years after their restoration, they staffed 266 establishments in France and thirty-six in Poland. Their number was 1580, of which 112 sisters served in the Maison-Mère in Paris.[22]

Monsieur Hanon knew of the study ordered by the Minister and tried to persuade the government of the rightness of his position. On 31 August 1808, in a long letter to Cardinal Fesch (the Emperor's uncle who served as Archbishop of Lyon and Grand Aumônier of the Empire) he explained that new regulations would represent unprecedented changes in the constitutions of the Daughters of Charity, and would expose this community (comprised of respectable and extremely useful women) to very dangerous problems that would undoubtedly lead to their destruction. He tried to explain that the Daughters of Charity had never had the status of nuns in a religious order, that rather they were a body of secular women who did not enjoy any of the privileges of nuns including exemption from episcopal authority. With regard to their interior life and spirit of their vocation, Vincent de Paul had provided that this would be maintained through their ties with the Congregation of the Mission. He pointed out that you could not remove this bond without destroying their Constitutions, their customary rules of conduct, their vows, and the unique spirit proper to their vocation of serving the poor.[23]

On 29 January 1809 Hanon wrote to the Minister of Cults and requested that his authority over the Daughters of Charity be confirmed by the government. He noted that this confirmation was necessary since the Daughters of Charity were preparing for their annual renewal of vows on the upcoming 25th of March. This renewal would include a renewal of their vow of obedience to the superior general of the Congregation of the Mission. He requested a speedy response to his letter noting that he needed time to also write to the sisters in Spain, Poland, Russia, and Austria.

The next day, in an interview with Cardinal Fesch, Hanon again defended the traditional ties between the Lazarists and the Daughters of

---

[22] AN: F/19/6247.

[23] AN: F/19/6344.

Charity.[24] In response to Monsieur Hanon's letter the Minister of Cults asked him to provide a copy of the brief that he held from the Holy See in regards to the Daughters of Charity, and a copy of the letter usually sent to the sisters for the renewal of vows. Monsieur Hanon sent a copy of the document from the Holy See on the 31st, but he noted that the letter for the renewal of vows had not yet been written, and would not be until after the response of the minister. He noted, however, that in general this letter usually "encouraged the piety of the sisters in living up to their vows."[25]

Hardening of the Conflict — 1809

On 18 February 1809, a new decree signed by Napoleon gave new directives to the congregations:

> 2. The statutes of each congregation will be approved by us and inserted into the Bulletin of the Laws.
> 3. All congregations, of which the statutes will not have been approved and published before 1 January 1810, will be dissolved.
> 6. Each hospital house, even the principal location if there is one, is under the jurisdiction of the diocesan bishop who will rule it, and will exclusively visit it. All superiors, other than the bishop in person, must be delegated by him and govern under his authority.
> 8. Vows must be professed in the presence of the bishop and the civil officer who will witness the act.[26]

The vicars general of Paris, who were charged with administering the archdiocese after the death of Cardinal Jean-Baptiste de Belloy in January 1809, also contributed their thoughts on the impact of this decree upon the Daughters of Charity:

> The government of the Gallican Church does not today have a subaltern ecclesiastical function independent of the authority of the bishops, nor one that is not submitted to the surveillance of our lords the bishops.... How unreasonable would it be to want a congregation erected by the archbishop of Paris with the charge of remaining in perpetuity under the

---

[24] *Ibid.*

[25] *Ibid.*

[26] AN: F/19/6310.

dependence and the jurisdiction of his successors, of which the superiors' only title is the commission and confidence they received to conduct and direct it, to be exempt, even in Paris, of the archbishop's jurisdiction?[27]

The sudden death of Mother Thérèse Deschaux on 17 April shocked the sisters. On the afternoon of that day, Monsieur Hanon, fearing without doubt the intervention of the vicars general, called together the council of the Company to take emergency measures. In virtue of article 9 of the statutes, which prescribed that the sisters name a replacement for the deceased superioress general while waiting for the election that would take place on the Monday following the feast of Pentecost, the members of the council named as their superioress general Sister Marie Antoinette Beaudoin (fifty-two years old, thirty-seven of vocation), at that time the sister servant at the Invalides in Paris. This election was ratified by the sister servants of Paris.[28]

After the promulgation of the 18 February 1809 decree, Cardinal Fesch asked the vicars general of Paris to modify the statutes of the Daughters of Charity in conformity with the Emperor's directives. The new statutes arrived at the Maison-Mère on Saturday, 6 May:

> Art. 2. The Company of the Daughters of Charity is not erected as a religious order but only as a congregation of women who obey, according to their Institute, Monsignor the archbishop of Paris as the superior general of the Company, or his delegate, and the one who is elected superior as well as the officers of the community.
> Art. 14. The superior will have the direction of all the Company as the delegate of Monsignor the archbishop. She will be like the soul of the whole body.
> Art. 16. The sisters, spread out in the departments, will obey our lords the bishops with respect to the interior discipline of establishments and the surveillance of spiritual administration.[29]

---

[27] Des Soeurs de la Charité en 1809 et 1810, AN: F/19/6344, text prepared by the archbishopric of Paris.
[28] D.C. Archives, book of elections; and AN: F/19/6344.
[29] AN: F/19/6240.

Jean-François Jalabert, one of the vicars general who sent the text, asked that it be immediately considered and accepted by the members of the sisters' council, and that it be returned by the following Wednesday.[30] Sister Beaudoin, the interim superior, was opposed to this new version of the statutes and refused to sign.

Monsieur Jalabert, who wanted to avoid a confrontation with the sisters, proposed that the Minister of Cults wait to take action until after the election, which was scheduled to take place the Monday of Pentecost, 22 May, in hopes that a more moderate sister would be elected. However, he did note that "we must convince stubborn heads."[31] Monsieur Bigot de Préameneu was impatient with the slow pace of negotiations. He demanded that Cardinal Fesch intervene immediately with the sisters:

> After the decree of 18 February I have several times reiterated the importance with proceeding toward implementing the reorganization of the Daughters of Charity so that they should be the first one recognized by the government. Three months have now passed. I have received letters from everywhere complaining that this delay keeps all of the Empire in suspense. I ask your Eminence to intercede and to terminate this affair without delay.... In the present circumstances, it would not be appropriate if the superioress general were nominated before the institution decree, which might come at any moment.[32]

Monsieur Hanon responded to the deadline imposed upon the sisters, and on 15 May he called a general assembly of the sisters living in the houses of Paris. At this meeting he proposed that they sign, anew, the old statutes. In the margins he wrote these remarks: "I the undersigned, attest that the statutes printed here are the only ones that have ever governed the Company and that they are word-for-word in accordance with the original held in the custody of Sister Beaudoin, interim superioress general of the Daughters of Charity, signed Hanon, Superior General of the Congregation of the Mission and the Daughters of Charity." On the evening of 15 May, Mother Beaudoin, accompanied by the sisters of the council, submitted the non-conforming statutes to the Minister of Cults. The minister refused to accept them.[33]

---

[30] *Ibid.*

[31] *Ibid.*

[32] AN: F/19/6344, text prepared by the archbishopric.

[33] *Ibid.*

Within the Maison-Mère, opinion was divided. Some sisters wanted to preserve the company at all costs and avoid a new suppression. They obtained signatures of a number of sisters to the amended statutes. Several days later this text was submitted to the Archdiocese of Paris.

On 24 May, Monsieur Jalabert informed the Minister of Cults that he had received the amended statutes of the Daughters of Charity "signed by some of those who inhabit the mother house." He noted, however, that the superioress "who, by virtue of her office has some influence in this affair is not among the signatories." Although a number of other sisters in Paris had not signed, he was satisfied. Jalabert thought things would fall back into place.[34] He read *The Life of Mademoiselle Le Gras* by Nicolas Gobillon, and undertook a study of the statutes promulgated by Monsieur Bonnet in the 18th century.

For his part the Minister of Cults was unhappy at the state of affairs. On 16 May he summoned Monsieur Hanon. The Minister's position was that on the basis of their 1655 approval, "At its origins, the congregation of the sisters had been put in perpetuity under the jurisdiction and dependence of the archbishop of Paris, and if the superiors of the Mission directed it, it was only because this role was conferred upon them, that is to say it was delegated to them by the archbishop."

Monsieur Hanon responded forcefully, sensing the consequences of any modification in the sisters' vow of obedience. "If the Daughters of Charity do not vow obedience to the superior of the Mission they will cease to be Daughters of Saint Vincent de Paul." He predicted that sisters would leave rather than submit to Episcopal authority which represented a violation of the moral relationship that existed between them and their superior (the superior general of the Congregation of the Mission). The Minister proposed a compromise, saying that Hanon could preserve his authority over the sisters by accepting it as a delegated role. Caught between the choice of agreeing to the decree or of being forcibly separated from the Daughters, Hanon asked for some time to consider the proposal.[35]

Monsieur Hanon's reactions were contradictory. He first said that he would resign as superior general but then he backtracked and accepted the delegation proposed by the Minister of Cults. In a letter of 19 May he informed Cardinal Fesch: "Monsignor, I told his Excellency the Minister of Cults that I would accept the delegation of Monsignor the archbishop of Paris for the conduct of the Daughters of Charity of Saint Vincent de Paul as proposed by Your Eminence. I take this opportunity to transmit this

---

[34] AN: F/19/6344.

[35] AN: F/19/6344, text prepared by the archbishopric.

decision to your Eminence as well, along with the assurance of my zeal and promptness in fulfilling these duties."[36]

But on 29 May, he repudiated delegation and again claimed total independence in governing the Company: "You cannot claim any rights with regard to the interior regime or the domestic and temporal government of the Company of the Daughters of Charity. That is the principal charge of the office of superior."[37]

The year 1809 also saw worsening relations between Napoleon and the Pope. Napoleon demanded that Pius VII honor the terms of the continental blockade he had instituted against his foreign enemies. When the Pope refused French troops invaded the Papal States on 2 October 1808, and quickly occupied Rome.

On 17 May 1809, the Papal States (located in central Italy) were incorporated into the French Empire. The Pope, on 10 June, excommunicated Napoleon. The reaction came swiftly. The Emperor arrested the Pope on 6 July and imprisoned him in Savonne, a port near Genoa in Italy. This action galvanized Catholic opinion against the Emperor.

As the wider conflict with the Holy See began, the struggle between Monsieur Hanon and the Minister of Cults also worsened. Laurent Philippe left Paris and traveled to the south of France. From there, on 8 July 1809, he sent a letter to a number of houses:

> At the mother house in Paris there is a grave disagreement among the sisters: some have preserved the respect and inviolable attachment to Saint Vincent and his statutes, and to his successor who is Monsieur Hanon. Others desire and ask for another superior, which would bring the ruin of the whole Company. That is why I now advise you to write to Sister Beaudoin, the interim superioress general, so she may tell her council of your attachment to the statutes of Saint Vincent and how much you are horrified by the proposed changes.[38]

In many houses this letter only served to create confusion. The sisters of Bazas said they would do whatever they needed to so that they could continue to take care of the sick. Those in Ussel wrote with embarrassment,

---

[36] AN: F/19/6240, and F/19/6344, text prepared by the archbishopric.
[37] *Ibid.*
[38] AN: F/19/6344.

that they did not understand the conflict.[39] One sister quickly sent a copy of the letter to the archbishop of Paris who, on 2 August, informed the Minister of Cults: "This letter is designed to create trouble and disturb the peace amongst the sisters."[40]

Climax of the Conflict — 1809-1810

On the advice of the Minister of Cults, the vicars general of Paris decided to suspend the profession of vows of the Daughters of Charity, as the question of who had the authority to approve their vows was not resolved. The order was dated 17 May 1809:

> Obedience vowed by the Daughters of Charity to the superior of the Mission is subordinate to that which is due to the archbishop of Paris, who according to canon law is their primary superior as confirmed by the original decree erecting said congregation.
> Art. 1. From this day, no more Daughters of Charity will be allowed to make vows until the legal approval of their Congregation.
> Art. 2. The vows made previously, even those to obey the superior of the Mission, are under the jurisdiction of the archbishop of Paris and during the vacancy of this see are under our jurisdiction.[41]

Resignation of the Superioress General, Mother Beaudoin — 10 July 1809

When this order was received on 10 July 1809, Mother Beaudoin decided to disobey its provisions. She authorized the young sisters in retreat at the Maison-Mère to pronounce their vows. She informed the vicars general of Paris of her actions, who in turn informed the Minister of Cults. Bigot de Préameneu was furious. He immediately suspended Mother Beaudoin from her functions as superioress general and ordered her to return to her former assignment at the Hôtel des Invalides in Paris. He named her assistant, Sister Marguerite Ithier, to replace her in governing the Company.[42]

Monsieur Hanon's reaction came swiftly. The same day, he wrote to the Minister of Cults. He said that the Minister's letter relieving Sister Beaudoin had been received, and had plunged the community into consternation. He

---

[39] *Ibid.*

[40] *Ibid.*

[41] AN: F/19/6240.

[42] AN: F/19/6319.

Félix-Julien-Jean Bigot de Préameneu (1747-1825).
Unsigned engraving.
Public Domain

expressed his surprise of the choice of Sister Ithier as superioress, since the rules did not call for the assistant to become superioress general, but rather called for a new election. Hanon admitted that the Company of Daughters of Charity was heading towards dissolution: houses were no longer sending postulants; and parents were urging their daughters to return home.[43] Of the 102 sisters who had entered the community in 1809, thirty had already returned to their families.

Mother Beaudoin obeyed the Minister's directive. She left the Maison-Mère and returned to Les Invalides. She informed Bigot de Préameneu:

> Sir, I am in receipt of the letter that Your Excellence did me the honor of writing. I have returned to the Hôtel des Militaires Invalides, as you ordered. At the direction of my superiors I recognize your authority, and I have been prompt in my obedience. However, sir, I do not believe that I have done anything to deserve this unjust treatment even though I can now fulfill my long held desire to return to Les Invalides.[44]

---

[43] *Ibid.*

[44] AN: F/19/6344.

Worried about this turn of events and fearing the departure of sisters from the hospitals, the vicars general, with the agreement of the Minister of Cults, rescinded the interdiction of the profession of vows for new sisters. And, to prepare for the election of the superioress general, the Minister asked for the minutes of past elections in order to verify the manner in which elections in the Company of the Daughters of Charity had been made.

Suppression of the Congregation of the Mission — 16 September 1809

Having been briefed on the situation, Napoleon would not stand for Monsieur Hanon's opposition. On 16 September he signed a decree suppressing the Congregation of the Mission. The information was sent to Sister Ithier, the interim superioress general: since the Congregation of the Mission no longer legally existed, Monsieur Hanon could no longer claim to be superior of the Daughters of Charity.

On 10 October, Jacques-Pierre Claude and Jacques-Pierre-Martin Braud were named respectively by the archbishop of Paris as superior and director of the Daughters of Charity. Monsieur Jalabert informed Sister Ithier: "The former attachment of these gentlemen to your congregation, their virtues, their experience, and the service they have given, provide the vicars general the confidence that this choice will be agreeable to you."[45]

At the Maison-Mère these nominations were not well received. The director of the seminary, Sister Pélagie Nicot, had the sisters of the seminary read Saint Vincent's conference on fidelity to the rules, especially this significant passage: "Never consent to any change whatsoever; avoid that like poison and say that this title of Confraternity or Society has been given to you so that you'll be steadfast in retaining the original spirit God gave your Congregation from its birth. Sisters, from the bottom of my heart I entreat you to do this."[46]

When, on 16 October, Monsieur Claude presented himself to the Daughters of Charity, he was not welcomed. As he entered the seminary all the sisters arose and cried: "Help! Wolf!" Revolt split the Company.

Imprisonment of the Vicar General — 29 October 1809

Persuaded that Monsieur Hanon would continue his opposition, Napoleon ordered his arrest. On 29 October 1809, he was imprisoned. At first, Monsieur Jalabert believed things would eventually calm down. Monsieur Hanon was freed in November.

---

[45] *Ibid.*

[46] 69. Fidelity to the Rules, 8 August 1655, *CCD*, 10:84.

Publication of the New Statutes — 8 November 1809

The process for the revision and approval of the statutes went on. On 1 November 1809, Monsieur Jalabert submitted these proposed modifications to Cardinal Fesch:

1. Add some of Monsieur Bonnet's statutes.
2. Add the following:
    – The Daughters of Charity are in conformance with the Imperial Decree of 18 February 1809.
    – The Congregation of the Daughters of Charity will be, and will remain in perpetuity, under the jurisdiction and dependence of the archbishop of Paris, conservator of the statutes. The archbishop will designate two priests to fill the function of superior and director respectively.
    – The sisters elsewhere in the departments are under the authority of the local Bishop.
    – The formula of vows contains this modification: I vow to obey our rules and our statutes for a year....[47]

These modifications were accepted by the government on 8 November 1809. By imperial decree Napoleon approved the statutes thus modified for the Daughters of Charity.

> Art. 1. The patent letters of November 1657, concerning the sisters of the hospitals of Charity, known as Saint Vincent de Paul, along with the letter of erection of the statutes and annexes, are confirmed and approved. The only exception are the dispositions relative to the superior general of the Missions (since the congregation was suppressed by our decree of 26 September) and the charge of said sisters to conform to the general rule of 18 February concerning hospitals, and above all the articles concerning Episcopal authority and the disposition of goods.
> Art. 2. The patent letters, the letter of erection and rule announced in the preceding article will remain in force and annexed to the present decree.
> Art. 3. The Daughters of Charity will continue to wear their usual habit and, in general, will conform above all

---
[47] AN: F/19/6344.

to the election of the superioress general and the officers, according to the laudable customs of their institution as they are expressed in said statutes written by Saint Vincent de Paul.

This decree became official when it was published in the *Bulletin des Lois* #252 (second trimester, 1809), article 4838. The text was sent to the Maison-Mère by Monsieur Achard, in the name of the vicars general of the archdiocese, with a very long explanation. Napoleon's actions were portrayed as being in accordance with Saint Vincent's thought:

> My dear sisters, we have as much satisfaction in seeing your statutes approved by his Imperial Majesty as you must have had in receiving them. You possess in your oratory the precious relics of Saint Vincent de Paul. Your institution is his good work. Your statutes are his masterpiece. His spirit, his body, his heart, all is among you and in your hands.
>
> The statutes that we gave you are not his work by a second hand, but his work. You will find his thoughts, his sentiments, and his inimitable style of tender and incomparable pity.
>
> Who would have thought, my very dear sisters, that the rule of 1718 would have made you forget the primitive statutes? The Minister of his Majesty discovered these with the perseverance that characterizes men of clairvoyance determined to find the truth in original documents. His Excellency found them in the archives of the former parlement of Paris, where Saint Vincent deposited them when he registered the patent letter. The Minister gave the originals to the Emperor who could clearly see the signatures of St. Vincent de Paul, the Cardinal de Retz and the patent letter. This was the original monument that the Emperor wanted to restore. Great men love to confirm the acts of other great men. The Emperor would not have found it worthy, worthy of Saint Vincent de Paul, worthy of your institution, to give you other statutes than the ones that Saint Vincent de Paul himself gave you.[48]

---

[48] *Ibid.*

The letter ended with an announcement of the date for the election of the superioress general, set for 10 December.

Election of Mother Mousteyro — 10 December 1809

This election was presided over by Monsieur Jalabert and Pierre Vignier, vicars general of Paris. One hundred forty-eight sisters were present and chose as superioress general Sister Judith Mousteyro, "even though she was somewhat opposed to the settlement albeit in a moderate way."[49] Mother Mousteyro was seventy-four years old (fifty-two years of vocation), and was the superior at the Clermont hospital. Sister Elisabeth Baudet (fifty-six years old, thirty-seven of vocation), superior at Ile de Ré, was named treasurer.

On 1 January 1810, Mother Mousteyro, in the customary new year's circular letter, sent the all the sisters copies of the new statutes and recommended the renewal of their vows. But on 4 January, conscious of the difficulties the vow of obedience to the bishop would cause to the life and work of the Company, she proposed an abbreviated formula to the vicars general based only upon obeying the rules.[50] The vicars general, after consulting Cardinal Fesch, refused the proposed formula and demanded that the vows include the statement of obedience to the rules and statutes — that is, obedience to the archbishop of Paris.[51]

In response Mother Judith Mousteyro wrote, 1 February, to the secretary of the archbishop:

Portrait of Cardinal Joseph Fesch (1763–1839),
Archbishop of Lyon, 1803-1839.
Public Domain

---

[49] D.C. Archives, book of elections.
[50] AN: F/19/6344.
[51] *Ibid.*

> It is impossible for me to express the surprise and sorrow caused to me by the text for formula of vows that you sent yesterday.... I flattered myself that I would be able reunite all our divided spirits. Which lead me to ask them to profess vows according to the formula I proposed. I hoped that this would be agreeable to you, since all we want is peace.... My conscience would reproach me for the rest of my life if I accepted such a formula.
>
> If we are forced to receive them it would be more proper for us not to renew our vows. This is what I would encourage the sisters to do, but in the end they will do what their consciences dictate.
>
> In my case, I have the advantage of having professed valid vows for forty years of my life. I cannot take back what I have already given to God.[52]

Without waiting for a response, Mother Mousteyro sent a circular letter to the sisters wherein she restated her opposition to all the changes in the Company's government. She was very conscious of the consequences this would have for her:

> At this time of year, I find myself in the position of not being able to send the traditional letter concerning the renovation of your vows. In light of the fact that the archbishop requires that we adopt a formula that directs our vow of obedience to him, I do not think that I have the power to consent for you, my dear sisters, and to make you agree to such a new concept, which would divide us from our sisters in Poland and other places. What is more, I would be remiss in the confidence that you have in me. And even if I am to suffer the same fate as Monsieur our Most Honored Father (Dominque Hanon), I would not agree to anything that would represent such an essential change to the work of Saint Vincent. On this point, I do not rely upon my own judgment, but believe that only the supreme authority (of the papacy) could change the words of our vow formula.

---

[52] AN: F/19/6344, text prepared by the archbishopric.

My dear sisters, let us renew our zeal and our charity towards our dear masters, the poor. The happy chains that attach us to their service are in no other hands than those of Jesus Christ.[53]

When he heard of Mother Mousteyro's decision Monsieur Jalabert went to the Maison-Mère of the Daughters of Charity to communicate the archbishop's disapproval and to try to make them submit.[54] Faced with the difficulties of his task, he proposed that the Minister of Cults exile from Paris all the sisters who were strongest in their support of the superioress general, in particular: the two directors of the seminary, Sister Pélagie Nicot (fifty-three years old, thirty-five of vocation) and Sister Gilette Ricourt (forty-nine years old, twenty-six of vocation); the superior of the parish of Saint Roch, Sister Françoise Tireau (sixty-four years old, forty-three of vocation); and the former superioress general, Sister Antoinette Beaudoin (fifty-three years old, thirty-eight of vocation).

On 19 March, Bigot de Préameneu sent for Mother Mousteyro. She visited the Minister of Cults accompanied by some sisters. It appeared at first that she was convinced by the Minister's arguments and that she was ready to accept the new vows of obedience. But, when she returned to the Maison-Mère, she reconsidered and wrote to the Minister that she would not accept the new formula of vows as she had led him to believe she would, and that she was prepared to tender her resignation. She admitted that she had originally agreed, but explained that she had felt pressured, and had been unable to express herself honestly.[55]

In a circular of 3 April 1810, Mother Mousteyro informed the Daughters of Charity that she had presented her resignation as superioress general:

> After long reflection in the presence of God, I have concluded that I must resign. When I accepted the role of superioress, I had some hopes that, with the grace of God, I could accomplish some good, in particular to bring about a union of all spirits as I had in other houses in which Providence had placed me. Now, after all the sacrifices I have made to bring peace, I no longer have anymore hope.

---

[53] D.C. Archives, and AN: F/19/6344.
[54] AN: F/19/6344, text prepared by the archbishopric.
[55] AN: F/19/6344.

I know that I have failed, and after all of the setbacks I have suffered, I am determined to resign. The final straw came when I was pressured to change the formula of our sainted vows; a change which would have cost me my conscience. The present situation makes it impossible for me to fulfill my functions as duty demands. I must ask God to give you light in the choice of a new superioress, because from this moment I no longer hold that position; I now see myself as the least member of the community.[56]

Election of Mother Durgueilh — 3 April 1810

The same day, two priests, Messieurs Viguier and Braud, came to the Maison-Mère of the Daughters of Charity and accepted the resignation of Sister Judith Mousteyro. In her place they appointed Sister Marie Dominique Durgueilh, superior of the Hospital of Saint Eloi de Montpellier. According to the custom of the Daughters of Charity, two sisters' names were proposed for election as superioress general. In the last election Sister Judith Mousteyro and Sister Durgueilh were chosen as the two candidates. The three sister councilors, Sister Marguerite Ithier, Sister Elisabeth Baudet, and Sister Marguerite Grange, along with the two priests of Paris, signed the register of election.[57]

Engraving of Jean-François Jalabert.
A vicar general in the Archdiocese of Paris,
Jalabert pushed for diocesan control of the Company.
Public Domain

---

[56] D.C. Archives.

[57] D.C. Archives, Book of Elections.

The archbishop of Paris immediately sent a circular to the Daughters of Charity affirming that calm had been reestablished, and asking them to follow divine inspiration and the wisdom of Saint Vincent in being faithful to their vocations.[58]

The next day, 4 April, Monsieur Jalabert informed the Minister of Cults of these developments. He told of Sister Mousteyro's resignation, and recounted that the directors of the seminary had been ordered to return to their families. He did not believe that Sister Mousteyro would encourage any further opposition amongst the sisters; he could not say the same however for Sister Nicot, who: "departed for Lyon where there are pockets of resistance," or of Sister Ricourt, who: "had departed to Mans where the sisters are very defiant." The local Bishop had been warned.[59]

On 15 May, Mother Durgueilh sent a circular letter to the Daughters of Charity informing them of her nomination as head of the Company. She said she had accepted the charge only to help preserve the community and avoid a new dissolution that would deprive the poor of the help of numerous sisters.

> Because I had been nominated at the last election, after the resignation of Sister Mousteyro the Lord called me to replace her, following the means approved by Saint Vincent I left the house to which I had been assigned to follow the demands of Providence. As hard as these sacrifices have been, I will do whatever I need to do to preserve our dear community. These are the only reasons that helped me, despite my repugnance, to decide to accept such a task, especially given the present circumstances. I have been greatly pained by the disunion that exists amongst us. While acknowledging the good intentions of many sisters, what they desire seems impossible. It is no less true, dear sisters, that we must not and cannot refuse to obey legitimate spiritual and temporal authority, as they do not ask us to do anything which is contrary to our holy religion. No community can survive in a State without the agreement and authority of both powers.[60]

The position taken by Sister Durgueilh was met by a range of reactions. If a good number of the sisters accepted the situation, some did so seemingly without understanding what was at stake. Others reacted negatively to her

---

[58] AN: F/19/6344.
[59] Ibid.
[60] D.C. Archives.

nomination. They refused to recognize the new superioress general, and did not accept the dismissal of the sisters who directed the seminary.

Approximately one third of the houses in France opposed the settlement. Almost 100 sisters decided to leave the Company. Among them, fifty had been in the community less than ten years. Many, particularly older sisters, had already rejoined their families once before during the dark years of the Revolution.[61]

Monsieur Hanon, who encouraged this resistance, was again arrested and imprisoned at the Fenestrelle Fortress in Piedmont. He remained there until Napoleon's defeat in April 1814.

On 1 March 1811, Mother Durgueilh sent the sisters the new vow formula:

> In the presence of God and of the Heavenly Host, I renew for one year my baptismal promises and make a vow to God of poverty, chastity, and obedience, in accordance with our rules and our statutes.[62] I also vow to dedicate myself in the Company of the Daughters of Charity, to the corporal and spiritual service of the sick poor, who are our true masters. I ask this by the merits of Jesus Christ crucified and through the intercession of the very holy Virgin.[63]

She urged the sisters to renew their vows as was customary on 25 March, the feast of the Annunciation: "I have put off writing to you about the renewal of our holy vows until I could send you the permission that you will find in this circular and the vow formula [...] I am persuaded, dear sisters, that it will be a great consolation to you to see the time of penitence that our Good Lord gave us last year come to an end. Its purpose, without a doubt, was so that we could appreciate his graces and accept his exhortation to a renewal of our fervor and fidelity."[64] Following this letter, the opposition hardened again. These sisters refused the new formula of vows which placed them under the jurisdiction of the bishops.

---

[61] Cf. AN: F/19/6344 — as of 18 December 1811.

[62] From the origins of the Company the formula read "I, the undersigned, in the presence of God, renew the promises of my baptism, and I vow poverty, chastity and obedience to the Venerable Superior General of the Priests of the Mission in the Company of the Daughters of Charity in order to give myself, for the whole of this year, to the corporal and spiritual service of the sick poor...." A.44B Formula of the Vows, *Spiritual Writings of Louise de Marillac*, ed. & trans. by Louise Sullivan, D.C. (Brooklyn, N.Y.: New City Press, 1991), p. 782.

[63] AN: F/19/6344.

[64] D.C. Archives.

Expulsion of Dissenting Sisters

Napoleon was surprised by the sisters' resistance. He reacted angrily and instructed Bigot de Préameneu to obtain the submission of all sisters: they were to indicate by oath or in writing their recognition of Mother Durgueilh, the superior named by the archbishop of Paris, upon the advice of the Minister of Cults.

The Bishops are Ordered to Take Action — March 1811

At the end of March 1811, the Minister of Cults sent a circular letter to the bishops: "His Majesty has learned that many sisters will not recognize the superioress general... The sisters who have refused to recognize their superior are not really Sisters of Charity... Not only must they submit, but if they cannot be persuaded to fulfill their duties they must be punished and publicly removed from the congregation."[65] In the following weeks numerous accounts of these efforts were submitted. Procedures to ensure the sisters' obedience had been put in place, either by the bishop himself, or by a priest delegated for the purpose.

The bishops' reactions were varied: some were submissive to the Emperor's orders while others defended the sisters. Cardinal Jean-Sifrein Maury of Paris was able to persuade Sister Bonamy, superior of the parish of Saint Paul, and Sister Beaucourt of the Invalides, but not Sister Tireau of the Parish of Saint Roch.[66] However, rebel sisters were not always welcomed in houses: "If the superior of Saint Paul, who has returned to the Maison-Mère, is not treated well her stubborn temperament will lead her to change her opinion which she had given out of the submission and respect due to your Eminence."[67] The bishop of Cahors announced the submission of the superiors of Cahors and of Montauban, but he noted that the superior of Agen was still insubordinate, "She travels around and stirs up trouble."[68] The bishops of Meaux, Coutances, Metz, and Evreux were able to obtain the submission of the sisters working in their hospitals and dioceses.[69] The bishop of Sees reported that it had taken him two hours to persuade the superior of Bellême. The bishop of Nancy related the distress of Sister Martel, superior of Verdun: "Will I violate my conscience if I recognize the new superioress general?"[70] The bishop of Versailles asked that the superior

---

[65] AN: F/19/6319.
[66] AN: F/19/6344.
[67] Ibid.
[68] AN: F/19/6319.
[69] Ibid.
[70] Ibid.

of the parish of Saint Louis be given special consideration in light of her zeal for service of the poor.[71] The bishop of Amiens insisted that the sisters be treated with kindness, acknowledging that "they exercise their functions with so much zeal and charity."[72] The bishop of Rochelle noted that the civil and military hospitals needed replacements for more than 50 sisters. "No sister is disposed to make their submission. It is against their conscience. Nothing will convince these hot-heads, particularly since they are women who are convinced that their faith is being compromised."[73] In Dijon and Lyon, the sisters also resisted efforts to have them submit.

Letters arrived at the Maison-Mère detailing the turmoil of conscience sisters were experiencing:

> I will not hide from you that I have had great trouble accepting the changes made to our statutes. I have finally accepted them, but not out of fear of the threats that have been made; the idea that these threats in-and-of-themselves would be capable of making me submit would be horrible to contemplate. It was the love of my vocation, and the fear of losing that, which were the only motives that persuaded me to submit to this new order of things of which I had such repugnance.[74]

> The love and respect that we had for our holy statutes led us to greatly desire that they should not be changed. However, in light of the governmental order which offers us the choice to either quit our vocation or accept the proposed changes, we declare that we adhere, being convinced that our adherence does not damage our conscience.[75]

After the intervention of the bishops 393 sisters out of 560 submitted, and twenty-six houses out of ninety-three declared their submission by recognizing Sister Durgueilh as superioress general and accepting the new vow formula.

---

[71] Ibid.
[72] Ibid.
[73] Ibid.
[74] Letter of Sister Dréan, hospice de Dax, 25 May 1811, AN: F/19/6319.
[75] Letter of the Community of the Hospital of Dax, 22 May 1811, AN: F/19/6319.

The Departmental Prefects are Ordered to Act — July 1811

Faced with the resistance of a number of sisters despite the intervention of the bishops the Minister of Cults Bigot de Préameneu, addressed the departmental prefects. In July of 1811 he sent a report on the dissident sisters within their various departments. He reminded the prefects that: "If the sisters refuse to recognize the superioress general, they must quit the habit and retire to their birthplace." Further, the minister demanded ongoing police surveillance: "The sisters sent away to their birthplaces are to be watched by the authorities so that they do not have any correspondence with the sisters of the congregation of Saint Vincent de Paul, of which they are no longer a part, and to ensure they do not exercise any function relative to their former positions as hospital workers."[76]

The prefects responded quickly, reporting the departures of the intransigent sisters. A report from November 1811, submitted by Mother Durgueilh at the request of the Minister of Cults, reported that eighty-seven sisters had chosen to leave rather than submit.[77] Some departmental prefects, such as those in La Rochelle, Rochefort, and Le Mans, dismissed local hospital sisters and requested replacements.[78]

The Bishops are Ordered to Act — January 1812

Faced with the continuing resistance of several houses, the Minister of Cults sent a new instruction to twelve bishops who would not, or could not convince the sisters, asking them to fulfill their orders. In some cases the bishops were able to obtain submissions, but more often than not the sisters remained firm in their opposition.

The bishop of Carcassonne informed the Minister that he had summoned the superior of Pennautier; Sister Marie Madeleine Chanu. The sister, old, infirm, and senile, arrived on a donkey. Despite her senility she told the bishop that she would not go against her conscience, even if they made her suffer. Her elderly companion responded the same way.[79]

The bishop of Béziers refused to implement the order of expulsion as the sisters in question were highly esteemed in the locality because of their good conduct and zeal in service to the sick. He explained that their expulsion would leave a bad impression.[80] The bishop of Toulouse reported on the eight houses in his diocese which contained seventy sisters. He

---

[76] AN: F/19/6319.
[77] AN: F/19/6344.
[78] AN: F/19/6319.
[79] Letter of 24 January 1812, AN: F/19/6319.
[80] Letter of 23 January 1812, AN: F/19/6334.

advised the Minister of Cults against any hasty actions, which could produce negative results.[81]

The resistance of the women surprised Napoleon, as an army general and Emperor he was accustomed to being obeyed. He hardened his tone in a new letter to his Minister on 3 March 1812:

> It is time to put an end to this scandal caused by the Daughters of Charity who are in revolt against their superior. My intention is to suppress all those houses which, despite the warnings you have given them, have not yet submitted. You will repopulate the insubordinate houses, not by sisters of the same order, but with those of another order of charity. The Daughters of Charity of Paris will thus lose their influence. That will be good. You will substitute sisters of an order which is more obedient and does not complain.[82]

New Actions by the Prefects — March 1812

On the same day as Napoleon's order, the Minister of Cults sent new instructions to eleven prefects. He recommended they unite speed with prudence in fulfilling their orders so there would be no interruption in the service of the sick in their hospitals. He asked them to call once more on the superior of each house and demand she cooperate in obtaining the submission of her sisters. But he recognized it would be difficult to replace the insubordinate sisters.[83] The next day he sent a letter to eleven other hospital congregations, asking for sisters to replace some 250 Daughters of Charity who had not submitted. Only five of the congregations responded, placing thirty sisters at the disposal of the minister.[84]

The prefects understood how difficult it would be to execute these orders. Those from the departments of the Basses-Pyrenees, Lot, Garonne, and Gers, asked permission to suspend the implementation of the orders given the difficulties their hospitals were facing in tending to the numerous sick and wounded Spanish prisoners. On 3 April, Bigot de Préameneu lost his patience and sent a new order to the prefects: "The insubordinate sisters represent an organized opposition which is very dangerous. The Emperor sees their resistance as a deplorable opposition to his government." An express order was given to expel the dissident sisters within twenty-four hours.[85]

---

[81] Letter of 28 February 1812, AN: F/19/6319.

[82] AN: F/19/6319.

[83] *Ibid.*

[84] AN: F/19/6344.

[85] AN: F/19/6319.

During the month of April 1812, 145 sisters received the order to leave their ministries, take off their habit as a Daughter of Charity, and return home to their families. They were each sent an internal passport. In several cases sick or elderly sisters could not travel and so some stayed and were cared for, while others were welcomed by friends. Some sisters had no family to return to. Where were they to go? Some asked to be allowed to rent a room nearby. Most often, they were allowed to do so.

Before their departures, many sisters again reaffirmed their determination to resist. The eight sisters of the hospital of Pau sent a letter to the bishop: "We do not want in any way to contribute to the destruction of the works of Saint Vincent, who often counseled us to resist any new innovations in our rules. If, faithful to these sentiments, we are found worthy of continuing in the service of the poor, we will be happy to do so. If the contrary is true, we will submit to the order of the government and leave."[86] At Trévoux, the five sisters signed a declaration affirming, "We leave the service of the sick with chagrin and sadness."[87]

The expelled sisters who returned to their families were placed under close police surveillance. The prefects had to certify that the former sisters no longer worked in hospitals, and that they were doing nothing to foment problems with the sisters who had submitted. The prefect of the department Loir et Cher noted that Sister Besnard, the former superior of the hospice of Mans, arrived in Saint Aignan, her birthplace, on 29 August, and that she was leading a tranquil life, did not wear the habit of the Congregation, and only dressed in black. The prefect of Allier noted that Sister de Boutin of the hospice of Saint Pol had not returned to Sauvagny, her place of birth. He believed she had retired in Enrichemont (Cher) at the home of her brother who was the town's priest.[88]

Some sisters would not accept their forced inactivity. Sister Louise Buyot, expulsed from Toulouse, went to work at the hospital of Muret under the pseudonym Dame Laventurier, the name of one of her father's lands. She was hired. Informed of this, the Minister of Cults demanded an explanation from the prefect of Toulouse: "This situation violates the orders of his Imperial Majesty. The Daughters of Charity who have not submitted must immediately relinquish the habit and be sent to their birthplaces."[89] On 18 August, the prefect of Toulouse confirmed the facts of the case, and he confirmed that the sister would be sent away.[90] In September, the prefect of Beaune was questioned by the Minister because the city's Welfare Bureau

---

[86] Letter of 11 April 1812, AN: F/19/6319.
[87] Letter of 19 April 1812, AN: F/19/6319.
[88] Letters of 30 September 1811, AN: F/19/6319.
[89] Letter of 28 July 1812, AN: F/19/6319.
[90] AN: F/19/6319.

had hired Sister Claudine Clavelot, originally of Beaune, to distribute public aid. The sister had been expelled from Sedan for being insubordinate and the prefect was then obliged to fire her.[91]

Since the beginning of the conflict almost 270 sisters had left or were expelled from the community. Among them, almost one third were sisters who had entered the Company of the Daughters of Charity after its restoration in 1801. This fact certainly illustrates the influence of the directors of the seminary, who after 1810 had publicly opposed all modification of the community's statutes.

Often local superiors encouraged the resistance in their communities. In Mans, Sister Besnard[92] led nineteen sisters in their opposition. In Béziers, Sister Amblard[93] led fifteen sisters who were expelled. In Lyon, twenty-two sisters were sent away to their families; in Toulouse, seventeen; in Dijon, fourteen; in Agen, eleven; in Auch, twelve; etc.…

Government of Mother Durgueilh — 1812-1814

Mother Marie Dominique Durgueilh, elected superioress general after the dismissal of Mother Mousteyro, was considered to be a usurper by the recalcitrant sisters. She was legitimately reelected by the sisters assembled according to the customs of the Daughters of Charity, on 18 May 1812.

On 22 February 1813, Pope Pius VII, imprisoned at the palace of Fontainebleau, signed a rescript confirming the powers of the superioress of the Daughters of Charity:

> Our Holy Father Pope Pius VII, considering the present state of the Congregation of the Daughters of Charity of Saint Vincent de Paul, and wanting good order and uniformity to be observed between the sisters as to the simple vows that they have to make each year, gives them all, under the present circumstances, the authority of professing, in accordance with their own consciences, the simple vows according to the commandment of the superioress general whom they must, according to the provision of their constitutions, recognize as the head of all the congregation.[94]

---

[91] *Ibid.*

[92] Sister Madeleine Besnard was named superioress general in May 1818.

[93] Sister Catherine Amblard was named superioress general in 1820, after the death of Sister Besnard.

[94] D.C. Archives.

Portrait of Pope Pius VII.
Painting by Jacques-Louis David (1748–1825).
Commissioned by Napoleon, 1805. Collection of the Louvre Museum.
Public Domain

On 7 March, Mother Durgueilh, after speaking privately with the Pope the night before, had the joy of attending the papal mass. She relayed the warm words of Pius VII to the sisters: "[…] I was presented to His Holiness, he received me with the greatest kindness. I asked for his blessing for myself and for all the community, which he kindly accorded because of our merit. I would not have thought to share his words if I did not want them to demonstrate the great affection that His Holiness has for the Daughters of Charity. This has given me hope that all those who have left will return." Mother Durgueilh was happy with the Pope's encouragement, interpreting it as his approval of her leadership of the Company.

The conflict the Daughters endured during these three years did not diminish the number of young women entering the community. In 1810, 110 were received in the seminary;[95] in 1812, 146; and in 1813, 127. The Maison-Mère, located on the Rue du Vieux Colombier, was too small to house all the novices. Mother Durgueilh asked the government for a bigger house.

---

[95] Name given to the Novitiate in the Daughters of Charity.

On 25 March 1813, an imperial decree conveyed the Hôtel de Châtillon, at 132 rue du Bac,[96] which belonged to the hospices of Paris, to the Daughters of Charity.

> Art. 1. The Hôtel de Châtillon, situated on the rue du Bac and belonging to the hospices of our good city of Paris, will be acquired by the city.
> Art. 2. The price of this house, valued at 26,000 francs, will be paid to the hospices by means of the surrender of a rent of 13,000 francs to be taken from profits at the wine market.
> Art. 3. Our good city of Paris will convey the house to the Daughters of Charity to function as the principal house of their order.[97]

A decree of the prefect of the Seine, dated 17 May, confirmed the sale of the Hôtel de Châtillon by the administration of the hospices of the city of Paris. "The Daughters of Charity will use freely, from this day, the Hôtel de Châtillon, to establish the principal residence of their order. This use will conform to the provisions of the Napoleonic Code relative to the rights of use."[98] Needed repairs were to be made by the city of Paris. The Ministry of the Interior granted a sum of 150,217 francs for the needed work.

After visiting the future location of the Maison-Mère, and in light of the growing number of vocations, Mother Durgueilh asked for the construction of a tribune for the chapel. The cost for this extra construction was covered by the sale of forty-six mirrors from the former Hôtel de Châtillon. A public sale was held on 13 February 1815, earning the sum of 7,683 francs.[99]

A Confusing Situation — 1814-1815

April 1814 brought profound political changes. During the War of the Sixth Coalition the allies invaded France in December 1813 and arrived in Paris, 31 March 1814. Napoleon abdicated on 11 April and left for the island of Elba. On 3 May, Louis XVIII, the oldest brother of the late King Louis XVI, entered Paris and restored the Bourbon Monarchy.

Napoleon's political prisoners were immediately freed. Pius VII left Fontainebleau and returned to Rome, where he was greeted with a triumphal

---

[96] The number later changed to 140 rue du Bac.
[97] AN: F/13/884.
[98] AN: F/13/740.
[99] *Ibid.*

welcome on 24 May. Dominique Hanon, who had been imprisoned since 15 February 1811, was freed on 13 April from the Fenestrelle prison. He obtained a passport for Lyon and arrived in Paris on 1 June 1814. He learned of everything that had taken place during his imprisonment. On 23 June he told the sisters:

> ...that he would immediately undertake the reestablishment of the community as prescribed by Saint Vincent. He asked them to forget about, and maintain absolute silence on, the events that had taken place over the last three years. He confirmed the decisions of Mother Durgueilh with regards to the foundation of new establishments; the nominations of sister servants; and placements of sisters. He retained Sister Chouilli as secretary general of the Company, and reappointed Sister Ricourt (a dissident sister who had left), as seminary directress replacing the current director, Sister Vincent. In addition, Mother Mousteyro, who resigned because she refused to accept the government's demands was to return as superioress general. Mother Durgueilh was to become her assistant. Finally he declared the election of 30 May as null and void, and directed that no other actions be taken until his arrival in Paris.[100]

When confronted by the Hanon's reproaches and directives, Mother Durgueilh justified her conduct:

> You are not unaware, my dear sisters, of the personal sacrifices I made when I left the house that was so dear to me. I made this decision upon the advice of enlightened persons — both the bishops and others — who urged me to make the sacrifices necessary to support the community which I was fortunate enough to return to peace and union. My authority was confirmed by the Holy Father in his rescript of 22 February 1813 [...] Our Most Honored Father has directed that I cede my office to Sister Mousteyro, aged seventy-nine years. He has notified her to this effect. However, I must note that her three year term of office has expired, and she was not re-elected two years ago. Our Most Honored Father has also replaced the directors of the

---

[100] D.C. Archives.

seminary and sisters staffing the secretariat with sisters who left the community several years ago. I foresee that this will lead to further troubles and divisions among us, and would afflict my heart which leads me to have no other attachment to my office than the best interests of the community....

At the end of the letter she added a postscript meant to reassure the sisters: "As my letter was written and sealed, I received orders from the king to remain in my position in the government of the congregation, without any changes or displacement in the Maison-Mère until the appropriate ecclesiastical authorities can make a definitive judgment."[101]

Monsieur Hanon replied in turn with a circular letter to the Daughters of Charity on 17 July: "I will not respond to the circular of Sister Durgueilh. Compare her letter to the one I wrote on 25 June." He reiterated the importance of Mother Mousteyro's return, and questioned the authenticity of the pontifical brief of 22 February 1813 to which Mother Durgueilh referred. The renewed polemic became a source of trouble and division.[102]

On 1 January 1815, Monsieur Hanon, wanting to rectify the situation, sent a very long circular to the Daughters of Charity in which he reaffirmed his role and his power as superior general and contested anew the legitimacy of Mother Durgueilh. He spoke at length of the sisters who had left, and took up their defense: "[…] The sisters who, during these three years, refused to recognize their new status because it was contrary to Saint Vincent's intent, suffered truly for justice and exercise an unquestionably legitimate defense of their status...."

The return of these sisters to the community was a long and complex process. During their absence, the sisters were replaced in institutions either by other Daughters of Charity, by sisters of other congregations, or by lay nurses. A careful and phased reentry was prudent for both order and justice.

Monsieur Hanon also addressed the sisters at length on the question of their vow formula. He criticized the wording imposed by the Archbishop of Paris which placed the sisters under the authority of the bishops. He ordered a return to the use of the traditional wording: "Your old formula, which almost all of you pronounced so many times with joy at the foot of the holy altar, correctly expresses your obedience to the venerable superior of the Congregation of the Mission, and was in use among you from the birth of your Company as placed there by Saint Vincent."[103]

---

[101] *Ibid.*

[102] *Ibid.*

[103] *Ibid.*

Mother Durgueilh replied, trying again to justify her actions:

> I have been made aware of Monsieur Hanon's circular. My conscience is not troubled because, by the grace of God, I have always, in regards to our affairs, acted only after asking for advice and after much prayer. But I am distressed by the thought that our sisters will accept this circular because this will involve us in a new set of troubles that will be even worse than the previous ones. The congregation will suffer in any case, and we will scandalize the world instead of edifying it. That is why I immediately write to ask you not to be troubled by this letter, and to exhort the sisters you know to not be worried.[104]

Papal Intervention — 1815

The situation facing the Community of the Daughters of Charity was fraught with difficulties. Monsieur Hanon's circular letters, which he had hoped would spur healing instead only made the wounds worse. Those of Mother Durgueilh, designed to justify the status quo, did nothing to calm the situation. Many letters were sent to Pope Pius VII asking him to intervene.

After studying the issues, the Pope tried to calm the conflict by naming Paul Thérèse David d'Astros, vicar capitular of Paris, as apostolic visitor for the Company of the Daughters of Charity, with all the rights traditionally accorded to the superior general. The pontifical decree was dated 17 January 1815.

On 20 February, Monsieur d'Astros sent a letter informing the sisters of his nomination. His first duty as apostolic visitor was to preside over the election of a new superioress general according to the statutes of the Daughters of Charity. Dominique Hanon would be allowed to be present. He was also to oversee the return of the dispersed sisters. The pontifical decree insisted on the restoration of unity among the sisters: "That their hearts should bind them in peace and charity, and that all things be reestablished in the old and good order and union; so that, reunited calmly and under the yoke of obedience, the Daughters of Charity may be strengthened in constancy and courage for the greater glory of God, the joy of the Church, and the advantage of Christians."[105]

Two days later Monsieur Hanon also sent the text of the pontifical decree, and added his commentary. He noted that more than 150 houses (out of 274) recognized his authority.

---

[104] *Ibid.*

[105] *Ibid.*

In March of 1815, Monsieur d'Astros convoked an extraordinary assembly of the Daughters of Charity for the new election of the superioress general. He demanded that all sisters participate in this assembly. On 12 March, the fifth Sunday of Lent, the assembly, brought together according to the rescript of Pius VII, elected as their superioress general Sister Elisabeth Baudet. Mother Elisabeth Baudet was not one of the dissenting sisters. She had served as the treasurer of the Company from 1809 to 1812 under Mother Durgueilh.

The evening of that same day, Monsieur d'Astros informed the sisters of the results of the general assembly and of the election of Sister Elisabeth Baudet. He noted that the election had taken place in the presence of Monsieur Hanon, who performed the functions assigned to him in the statutes. The apostolic visitor called for all of the dissident sisters to return to the community. These individuals were to write to the superioress, who would "take care of the manner, the place, the time for the sisters' return, and their new assignments as she deemed fit."

The following Tuesday, Mother Elisabeth Baudet announced her election as superioress general: "Be sure, my dear sisters, of my willingness to continue to achieve peace and union among us. I hope that you will make this task easier for me by renewing your fervor in the practice of perfect charity, in your regularity, and your zeal in serving the poor."[106]

However, the calm which was gradually returning to the Company of the Daughters of Charity took a sudden and unexpected turn. On 20 March, Napoleon Bonaparte, who had escaped the island of Elba where he was prisoner, entered Paris, and was welcomed by the populace. Louis XVIII escaped to Gand, in Belgium. As Monsieur Hanon would say a few months later, "This return puts us in great peril, and causes us consternation and alarm."

Napoleon's presence was short lived: 100 days. The defeat at Waterloo, 18 June, brought his downfall. Followed to Paris by the victorious armies, Napoleon signed his second abdication 22 June 1815. He was then deported to the island of Saint Helena.[107]

The presence of allied soldiers around Paris frightened the sisters in charge of educating young girls at the house of Saint Cyr. It was decided to send the girls to Paris for safety, and to house them at the Rue du Vieux Colombier. On 29 June 1815, the Daughters of Charity vacated their house on the Rue du Vieux Colombier and moved to their new Maison-Mère, at the Hôtel de Châtillon, on the Rue du Bac, where construction was

---

[106] *Ibid.*

[107] Napoleon died on Saint Helena, 5 May 1821.

Napoleon on his imperial throne.
Painting by Jean-Auguste Dominique Ingres (1780–1867).
Oil on canvas, 1806. Collection of the Musée de l'Armée.
Public Domain

almost complete. The move was quickly accomplished. The remains of their founder, Louise de Marillac, arrived first, then the seminary directresses and the 100 seminary sisters after, and finally the sick and infirm sisters. On 6 August, Monsieur Hanon blessed the chapel of the new Maison-Mère, a chapel requested from the government by Mother Durgueilh.

Return of the Expelled Sisters

The reentry of the dissident sisters of the Company posed some problems. Should the sisters return to the houses they had left in 1811 and 1812, or should they come first to the Maison-Mère in Paris? Would they be welcomed by a community divided by their departures? Tensions remained high in the Company as positions were taken on both sides.

On 1 January 1815, Monsieur Hanon wrote in his circular letter to "our sisters, who have been the victims of impious challenges to the authority and the institutions of the Church." He affirmed that they would be called back to "their offices, to the places and houses of the Company, as soon as it will be possible." While waiting, he asked them to remain in their current locations. He affirmed that sisters could return to their original houses if the sisters living there welcomed them. However, he also affirmed: "But those returning to their old houses must see this as only a temporary situation. They will be responsible to the local superior who will inform us of their return. The fact that they resisted Napoleon, and defended the link between Company of the Daughters of Charity and the Congregation of the Mission, will not give them any special rights or power."

In the decree of 19 February 1815, naming the apostolic visitor, Pope Pius VII expressed his wish that "all the dispersed sisters be called back to the family; that hearts be reunited by the ties of peace and charity and that all things be reestablished in good order and unity."

Napoleon's 100-days-return created another interruption. On 16 October 1815, Monsieur Hanon gave new directives to facilitate the return of sisters to the Company: "We desire that everyone, without exception, reenter houses of the Company by All Saints Day. Here are the steps to be taken to execute this measure which we announce after having relayed them to the dear sister superioress general and her council."

> All our dear dispersed sisters who, at the reception of the present circular, have not yet been assigned to a particular house will be able to re-enter without delay at any house where the sister servant will receive them until a definitive assignment can be made, if their infirmities or their age are not an obstacle. If they have received no invitation to a particular house, they may seek to enter at any convenient house, and the sister servants are authorized to receive them and offer them all possible assistance. If any outcast sister is not invited, contacted, nor accepted by a house, as described above, she may contact us in Paris where we will find a place as soon as possible.

Old or infirm sisters were authorized to join their former houses if the sister servant would accept them.

Monsieur Hanon ended his circular by insisting on the necessity of everyone coming to a great union of heart and minds:

But what would be the use, dear sisters, of submitting to the authority of your legitimate superiors if you still remain divided among yourselves? What would be the use dear sisters, if your faith does not fill your hearts now with the charity and humility that will enable you to forget mutual wounds, soothe and silence your feelings, and allow the attentiveness and kindness of the truly religious friendships which characterized your pious ancestors and made them only one family, one heart, and one mind in the Lord? Pardon! ... Forget! ... Remove from your hearts everything that disposes you to bitterness.[108]

A reading of the registers of the Company of the Daughters of Charity reveals that the return of these sisters took place over several years, and that in the end only a small number of sisters never returned. A dozen aged sisters died at home with their families between 1812 and 1816. About twenty, generally young women who entered after 1810, did not come back to the Company and decided to leave definitively. However, the great majority of sisters came back to the Company and again took up their community life and service of the poor. While some returned in 1814 and 1815, some waited until 1816, and a small number did not return until 1817 and 1818. The registers do not indicate the reasons for these delays. For some sisters, only the fact of their return is mentioned and there is no date specified.

When Monsieur Hanon died on 24 April 1816, the divisions within the community were still very much alive. This entire period has been described as a "schism." But who were the schismatics? The sisters who left, or those who remained? Who was right? Who was wrong? Those who defended the dependence of the Daughters of Charity, on the jurisdiction of the superior general of the Congregation of the Mission, or those who wanted to maintain the life of the Company when it was threatened with destruction? The tensions and outlooks which arose through the differing approaches to these questions took a long time to dissipate. The Daughters of Charity had to learn to accept one another though their opinions in the past might have differed, and be reconciled with one another. The new vicar general, Marie-Charles-Emmanuel Verbert, reiterated the "call to flee from discord, to return to a tender Christian friendship."[109]

---

[108] D.C. Archives.

[109] C.M. Archives.

Conclusion

"The crisis that rocked the Company of the Daughters of Charity shows the growing interest of the State in the direction of religious congregations."[110] Desiring to have personnel to staff the empire's hospitals and hospices, Napoleon restored the Company of the Daughters of Charity. His only concern was the social utility and effectiveness of this congregation. Desiring to solidify his power, he wanted to place all women's religious orders under the jurisdiction of those bishops whom he would choose.

The resistance of these women took him by surprise, particularly as a man who commanded the armies of the Empire with such success. Napoleon, in some regard, tolerated "this scandal." Usually, those who resisted him — the Pope, bishops, military men — were immediately arrested and imprisoned. Napoleon was less severe in his punishment of the women: he was content to send them home! And so the sisters returned to their families resolved not to give in to this man who had so disrupted the identity of the community.

This crisis demonstrated the difficulty of interpreting official texts. The juridical authority of the Company of the Daughters of Charity was subject to different interpretations, some demanding a literal reading others taking into account traditional practices. It also illustrated that women were capable of obstinately defending their point of view, despite the threat of governmental reprisal. It revealed that the vow of obedience taken by the sisters did not suppress their ability to judge matters in accord with their consciences. Certainly, among themselves the Daughters of Charity interpreted events differently. They expressed their points of view and took opposing sides. Their decisions created tensions, and even conflict within the community. As in any society, time was needed to heal, and erase, the memories of past suffering.

The statutes of the Daughters of Charity, signed by Napoleon on 7 November 1809, remain without modification the official text with respect to the administrative relationship between the French State and the Company of the Daughters of Charity.

On many occasions since this time, the Church has reaffirmed the ties existing between the Congregation of the Mission and the Company of the Daughters of Charity, and confirmed the jurisdiction of the superior general of the Congregation of the Mission. The constitutions of the Daughters of Charity, as revised and approved by the Church in 1983, declare:

---

[110] According to Jacques-Olivier Boudon, president of the Napoleon Institute (http://www.institut-napoleon.org/).

Since its origin, the Company has willed to be subject to the authority of the Superior General of the Congregation of the Mission, the successor of Saint Vincent de Paul. He has over the Company the double power, dominative[111] and jurisdictional,[112] recognized by the Church and by the Constitutions.

The Daughters of Charity acknowledge and accept him as God's representative, the one who helps them to maintain their characteristic spirit and to carry out their mission in the Church. They vow to obey him, and he may command them in the name of this vow. Everything in the Company that pertains to vows is within his competence.[113]

---

[111] Power of the superior to direct and give orders for the common good, according to universal and specific norms of the law.

[112] Public and ecclesiastical power to govern one's subjects internally and externally, according to universal and specific norms of the law.

[113] Constitutions and Statutes of the Daughters of Charity (1983): C. 3.27, page 69.

Saint Louise de Marillac's Uncle: Louis XIII's Garde des Sceaux, Michel de Marillac (1560-1632)

By

Donald A. Bailey, Ph.D.

The name Louise de Marillac, writes Louise Sullivan, D.C., "has largely remained hidden" in the "shadow" of her famous mentor and colleague, Vincent de Paul.[1] A similar shadow has, until recently, hidden the reputation of Saint Louise's uncle, Michel de Marillac (1560-1632), despite being arguably among the half-dozen most important political figures during the reign of Louis XIII. But in her uncle's case the shadow was deliberately created by Cardinal Richelieu, who did his best to obscure the memory and anti-war sentiments of his sometime collaborator and ministerial colleague.

At the time of his disgrace, Michel de Marillac was effectively what today we would call the Minister of Justice (in American terms, the Attorney General). He had served in the Royal Council since 1624, for two years as co-*Surintendant des Finances*, and during the following four-and-a-half years as *Garde des Sceaux* — that is, the Keeper of the Seals, appointed to take over all the responsibilities of drafting and adjudicating French law from an out-of-favor, but irremovable, Chancellor. To these posts he brought great intelligence, probity, financial integrity, courage, strong (but perhaps still vague) aspirations for government reform, and immense experience.

He had spent almost a decade as a Councillor in the Parlement de Paris, over fifteen years as a Master of Requests (the king's principal bureaucratic team for administration and justice, reinforcing the royal will throughout the kingdom and reporting back with their on-site observations), and approximately twelve years as a Royal Councillor primarily focused on financial matters.[2] More remarkably, he had compiled two still unpublished,

---

[1] Louise Sullivan, D.C., "Louise de Marillac: A Spiritual Portrait," in *Vincent de Paul and Louise de Marillac: Rules, Conferences, and Writings*, ed. Frances Ryan, D.C., and John E. Rybolt, C.M. (New York: Paulist Press, 1995), 39.

Last year, 2010, marks the 350th anniversary of the deaths of these partner saints, and the joint celebration of this date should help in shedding greater light upon Louise.

[2] Marillac's personal life and political career: birth, 28 August 1560; loss of mother, 1568, and of father, 1573; *conseiller lai au Parlement de Paris*, 3 September 1586; marriage to Nicole, *dite* Marguerite, Barbe de La Forterie (1561-1600), 12 July 1587; three surviving children; *maître des requêtes* 24/5 January 1595; widowhood, 1600, then second marriage, to Marie de Saint-Germain (widow of Jean Amelot), September 1601; *conseiller d'État*, 1612; enters *Conseil d'État*, November 1612; a *conseiller des finances*, 1619; co-*surintendant des finances* (with Jean Bochart de Champigny), 27 August 1624; *garde des sceaux*, 1 June 1626; proclamation/publication of the *Ordonnance du Roi Louis XIII...* (the "Code Michaud"), January 1629; disgrace and arrest, 12 November 1630; death at Châteaudun, 7 August 1632.

but often copied, treatises that were virtually archives / handbooks of the offices and functions of the Royal Council, with special attention given to questions of finance and justice. Two years before his disgrace, he wrote and edited the largest single codification of French law before (and even including) Napoleon's famous codes, <u>and</u> prepared yet another treatise to blunt the inevitable challenge he knew his code would face from the *Parlement de Paris*.[3]

As we shall illustrate in a moment, Marillac was also a zealous, pious, and devout Catholic. But, not only was he a prominent and influential *dévot*; he was the virtual leader of what was known as *le parti dévot*, that is, the persons and aspirations of the French Catholic Reformation as it involved itself in domestic and foreign political affairs. Because of the all-pervasive intimacy of Church and State in Late- and Post-Medieval Europe, neither Church nor State could be much reformed or influenced without involvement in the other too. At least since the Concordat of 1516, royal appointments to all principal religious offices had been more at the discretion of the French king than under papal control; in addition, political and social affairs were administered as much through ecclesiastical channels as through governmental ones, whether municipal, provincial, or royal, and secular officials continually intruded upon religious and ecclesiastical matters.

Engraving of Louis XIII (1601-1643).
Public Domain

---

[3] These treatises bear the titles *Des Chanceliers et Gardes des sceaux de France, du pouvoir et usage de leurs charges et de leurs droitz des sceaux et de la cire*; *Recueil des Conseils du Roy, et l'origine et règlemens d'iceux. Ce recueil contient seulement des exemples tirez de l'antiquité, de l'histoire et des registres de Parlement et autres, de ce qui s'est observé cy-devant en chacun des articles remarquez et contenus en iceluy*; and *Mémoire dressé par le garde des sceaux de Marillac, principalement contre l'authorité du Parlement*. At least one copy of each can be found at the Bibliothèque nationale de France [BnF] (rue Richelieu site), with additional copies of the latter two, also elsewhere.

Marillac and his half-brother were both relatively close to Marie de Medici, wife, then widow, of Henry IV, and mother of Louis XIII. A secondary diplomatic and military figure, Louis de Marillac had, in fact, married a very distant cousin of the Queen's,[4] and was to play fairly prominent roles in all of the young Louis XIII's military campaigns against the French Calvinists (a.k.a. the "Huguenots"). He was eventually elevated to become one of the marshals (*maréchaux*) of France. Both Marillacs helped Richelieu's return to power in early 1624, and were in turn raised to more prominent posts themselves. All three, as well as the Queen Mother, shared the king's desire to weaken, even eliminate, the Huguenot presence in France, to reform and strengthen the French Catholic Church, and — at least in the case of Cardinal Richelieu and Michel de Marillac — to reform diverse aspects of the financial, administrative, and judicial institutions and practices of royal government.

Corruption, inefficiencies, incompetence, and insouciance towards royal authority were all objects of their reformist concerns — so many concrete examples, yet the myriad of impediments to reform meant that conceptualizing a real program necessarily remained frustratingly vague and erratic. With the 1620s came the gradual beginnings of change, dramatically in the case of Protestant heresy, more tentatively as regards the reshaping of government. Finance, administration, justice, social status, and family connections — as well as the same ecclesiastical considerations — made it equally difficult to formulate and implement reform. But the place and security of France on the European stage was also of importance, and Spanish imperialism, even if considerably disguised as the agent of the Catholic Counter-Reformation, could not be ignored by French statesmen.[5] Challenges from Spain and the Empire to the Mantuan inheritance by an Italian-descended French nobleman (Charles de Gonzague de Nevers) could not be ignored, especially since Mantua was strategically important in the upper Po valley.

Richelieu and the king were also committed *dévots*, but they allowed potential threats to French interests abroad to distract them from their domestic religious and political reform objectives. They tried to keep Michel de Marillac and the Oratorian founder, Pierre de Bérulle (who was to die in 1629), well informed about the realities of Spanish ambitions, but both men continued to minimize the danger from Spain while emphasizing the

---

[4] This Catherine de Medici happened, in fact, to be a closer relative of the recent, third Florentine Medici pope, Leo XI (27 days in April 1605), than was the Queen herself. The marriage to Louis de Marillac took place in 1607.

[5] An historian of true objectivity would not note the 20th-century parallel here to Soviet imperialism with its disguise of communism, without also noting the equally evident phenomenon of American imperialism disguised with capitalist-related democracy.

urgency of finishing off the Huguenots at home, and strengthening royal authority overall. It was Marillac's persistent objections to the war that led to his disgrace in early November 1630. Louis de Marillac, too, marshal since June 1629 (and one of three generals in command of this very Italian campaign), was summarily arrested, tried in a fixed court, and executed in 1632. Had the *dévots'* insistence on reform prevailed (and the Ordonnance of 1629 not been still-born), the French Revolution might have been avoided, but such speculation is off limits for the professional historian!

Having briefly sketched Marillac's political involvements, we are now free to look at his intellectual and devotional activities, which were perhaps even more remarkable. All aspects of his life and career were thoroughly consistent with those of his ancestors, who — sometimes within the career of a single individual — were to be found in both the political and ecclesiastical arena. Tracing back five generations, a putative paternal ancestor is claimed to have married the equally problematic Antoinette de Beaufort de Canillac, the supposed niece of Pope Gregory XI and grand-niece of Pope Clement VI. Each of these popes played a central role in the history of the fourteenth-century Avignonese Papacy.[6] Over four generations, one or more Marillacs was either a secretary or financial official to various members of the Bourbon family — a fact which should not be overlooked in seeking to explain why a zealous Catholic Leaguer such as Michel de Marillac was eventually persuaded to embrace the not-yet-converted Henry of Bourbon-Navarre as his rightful king in 1593.

Michel had nine uncles and two aunts, whose involvements in military, administrative and/or religious careers ranged from noble service in the family's native Auvergne and other provinces to royal service in the Parisian capital or wherever else the king had need of them. To take but two examples: Charles de Marillac (ca. 1500-1560) was abbot of Saint-Père-les-Melun, bishop of Vannes in Britanny, and then archbishop and count of Vienne in Dauphiné; but he had also undertaken diplomatic tasks in Constantinople,

---

[6] Admittedly this takes us at least one generation further than where some Marillac genealogists are willing to be certain of the lineage, but the Marillacs themselves may well have embraced such claims, and so they form part of the family's self-understanding. Anne-Valérie Solignat, "Les généalogies imaginaires des Marillac ou comment faire des siens des gentilshommes de noblesse immémoriale," a paper presented to research colleagues at "Penser l'édition numérique critique: *La Vie de Michel de Marillac* par Nicolas Lefevre de Lezeau — Première journée d'études — Nicolas Lefevre de Lezeau et l'écriture" (23 March 2011).

It was Clement VI who in 1348 purchased Avignon outright from its previous *seignieur*, Queen Joan of Naples; and Gregory XI, who was in 1377 persuaded by Saint Catherine of Sienna to move the papacy back to Rome.

Interestingly, the spirituality of this Catherine of Sienna was to appear in Louise de Marillac's mature writings. Http://fr.wikipedia.org/wiki/Louise, p. 1 (accessed 12 July 2010).

England, and the Holy Roman Empire, as well as eventually capping various judicial activities with membership in the king's Privy Council. His brother, Guillaume II (ca. 1518-1573), Michel's father, was knighted on the field of battle and capped a long career in royal administration by becoming Comptroller-General of Finances (*contrôleur général des finances*) about five years before his death.[7] The religious commitments of this generation are further revealed in mentioning a third brother's becoming bishop of Rennes,[8] an aunt's being a Dominican nun (and poet) at Poissy, and yet another brother's being disinherited on account of his conversion to Calvinism and subsequent flight to Geneva.

With such a family history it is intriguing that not one of Michel's siblings entered the religious life, even if he himself made two futile attempts as an adolescent. Nonetheless, his own descendants did so in abundance, and at least one male in each generation followed the family tradition of a secular judicial/administrative career too. His daughter, widowed daughter-in-law, three granddaughters, and a great-granddaughter all became Carmelites. Two brothers of this youngest Carmelite became priests, one of them gaining some prominence in intellectual and pious pursuits.[9] Marillac's younger son became a Capuchin (who was nominated to the see of St-Mâlo at the time of his death) and his elder grandson, a Knight of Malta. Except for her prominence and sanctity, Saint Louise de Marillac must be seen as a thoroughly typical member of this extended family, especially when one considers other religious and several zealously pious laymen and -women among Michel's nieces, nephews, and cousins. Here, we find another bishop of relative prominence, as well as persons actively supporting the Company

---

[7] It is remarkable how uncertain so much scholarship remains. A major concern for me during the fifteen or so years of working on the Marillacs' genealogy has been consistently turning up either nothing, or else approximate dates for these two important brothers: until recently "ca. 1510" for Charles, and "ca. 1500" for his "younger" brother Guillaume II. Then, I found (without cited sources) that Charles' birth has been assigned ca. 1500, and Guillaume's ca. 1518. What to think?

[8] This brother, Bertrand de Marillac, is among those "reforming bishops" cited in J. Michael Hayden and Malcolm R. Greenshields, *Six Hundred Years of Reform; Bishops and the French Church, 1190-1789* (Montreal & Kingston: McGill-Queen's UP, 2005), Appendix 4B-2, p. 379.

[9] This outstanding priest was Louis de Marillac (d. 25 February 1696), *docteur de Sorbonne*, *curé* of Saint-Germain-l'Auxerrois (1670-94) and then of Saint-Jacques-la-Boucherie (1694-96). Also prior of Langeay (or Langey or Langeais), he opened two houses for young monks to meet together with ecclesiastics for pious exercises; in his home, he built a chapel and a cavern for devotions, and this home became a seminary under the name of Saint-Pierre and then Saint-Louis. Being made *Supérieur* of the Regular Clerks of Saint-Paul in 1669, he associated his community with that of the Pontoise Carmel. (For supporting references, see my edition of Nicolas Lefèvre de Lezeau, *La vie de Michel de Marillac (1560-1632)* [PU Laval, 2007], p. 517.)

of the Holy Sacrament,[10] a new group long dreamed of by Michel de Marillac and his *dévot* associates, but only realized on the eve of his disgrace. Amongst several "zealous and effective assistants of Louise de Marillac," Louis Châtellier mentions a "Mademoiselle Hardy,"[11] who may well be Françoise le Hardy, marquise de Flamarens, a granddaughter of Louis and Michel's elder sister Marie de Marillac Hennequin and thus actually a second cousin to Saint Louise herself. Mademoiselle Hardy was one of those who "vigorously solicited Vincent de Paul on behalf of orphans."

Before addressing the relationship between Michel and his niece, however, let us turn to the uncle's myriad devout activities. First, his personal zeal for prayer, discipline, and frequent communion. If I may be permitted to quote myself from a recent article:

> Well before his entry into high office, Marillac attended all matins in his parish on feast days and Sundays. He practiced the austerities and spiritual mortifications of the Catholic Reformation in France: sleeping on the tile floor of his *hôtel*'s chapel, refusing a feather bed when deteriorating health forced him off the tiles, remaining up late into the night, frequent fasting, etc. He even wore "a belt of small silver bow knots" — that is, a sharply studded girdle around his waist, from which many zealous penitents occasionally sustained bloody wounds. And he often used the "discipline" — a short whip of cords or small chains with which extremely devout persons flagellated themselves.[12]

Marillac had become a Grey Penitent around 1590 and was eventually successful, in 1594, in being elected church warden (*marguillier*) of his parish of Saint-Gervais. Already alluded to was his zeal in serving the Catholic League at the end of the French Religious Wars, before his preference for law

---

[10] These are children of Michel's half sister Valence de Marillac and her husband Octavien II Dony d'Attichy (*surintendant des finances* for Marie de Medici): Louis Dony d'Attichy (1598-1664), a friar of the Minim Order and then bishop of, first, Riez, then, Autun; and Anne Dony and her husband Louis de Rochechouart, count of Maure, both of whom actively supported the Company of the Holy Sacrament while never hiding their animosity towards Cardinal Richelieu, who had so brutally treated Anne's uncle, Marshal Louis de Marillac. Two other children of Valence and Octavien Dony give us another Carmelite and a Jesuit.

[11] Châtellier, *The Europe of the Devout: The Catholic Reformation and the Formation of a New Society*, trans. Jean Birrell (Cambridge: Cambridge University Press, 1989), p. 103.

[12] "Power and Piety: The Religiosity of Michel de Marillac," *Canadian Journal of History / Annales canadiennes d'histoire* 42:1 (Spring-Summer / printemps-été 2007): 8. (The article was reprinted, slightly revised, in *Vincentian Heritage* 28:1 [2008]: 33-56.)

and order, acceptance of the sincerity of Henry IV's promises to convert, and perhaps his family's long association with the House of Bourbon persuaded him to support the still beleaguered king.

His principal achievements, however, were his extraordinary services on behalf of newly founded reform monastic orders in France and his meticulous, spiritually sensitive translations of Thomas à Kempis's *Imitation*

Portrait of Michel de Marillac (1560-1632). Engraving by Michel Lasne.
Image Collection of the Vincentian Studies Institute

of Christ and the biblical *Psalms*. Both of these translations enjoyed two or more editions, and the former was a virtual best seller for a good part of the century; it was even twice reprinted in the nineteenth century. Marillac also wrote a treatise on the extent of papal authority over the French Church, and a history of the founding and early years of the French Carmelites.[13] While under house arrest at Châteaudun, he translated the *Book of Job* and left unfinished his long-in-process "Treatise of the Eternal Life."

Just as the gestation of the reformed, Teresian Carmelites in France was budding, Marillac arrived to assist in the ultimate flowering of their establishment. At this point his fertile hands were everywhere. Beginning with the first convent in Paris in 1604, he handled or actually drafted the papers requiring royal and then papal approval for each new house. Both in Paris and in Pontoise, he helped locate the sites and supervised the workers effecting necessary renovations. He ordered furnishings and supplies, and at every stage provided financial guarantees, actual loans, and even generous gifts, these last sometimes involving dowries for worthy novices from modest backgrounds. Together with Barbe Acarie, he could even be found counselling young novices, a task in which his command of Spanish was often called upon to facilitate the direction expected from Teresian Carmelites recently arrived from Spain. In fact, the first prioress at Pontoise found the ubiquitous pair of Acarie-Marillac rather intrusive, despite her appreciation of their piety and dedication.[14]

By my count, in 1618 there were twenty-two reformed Carmelite convents in France, and it was becoming necessary to defend the future of their independence from the late-arriving (1611) Carmel Fathers. The Fathers oversaw Carmelite convents in some countries, but not in others, and from the beginning Marillac had sought their assurance that they would not try to interfere with the French establishments. Insisting upon this story was one reason, no doubt, for the book he wrote in 1622 on the Carmelites' earliest years in France.[15] In the meantime, he also collaborated with Madame Acarie

---

[13] The former work is *Examen du livre intitulé Remonstrance et conclusions des gens du Roi, et arrest de la cour de Parlement du vingt-sixième novembre M.D.C.X., attribué faulsement à M. Servin, conseiller du Roy en son Conseil, et son advocat en la cour de Parlement de Paris, comme ayant esté faicte en ladicte cour sur le livre du cardinal Bellarmin, pour monstrer les ignorances, impertinences, faulsetés et prévarications qui se treuvent presque en touttes les pages*. N.p.: N.p., 1611.
For the latter work, see footnote 15.

[14] This was Anne de Saint-Barthélemy (1549-1626), one of the Spaniards who had been especially close to Saint Teresa of Avila herself. We hope for the imminent publication of the papers presented at the colloquium celebrating the 400th anniversary of the Monastère de Saint-Joseph at Pontoise: "Le Carmel: quatre siècles à Pontoise 1605-2005" (19-20 Novembre 2004). My presentation was titled, "Michel de Marillac et le Carmel de Pontoise" (presented 19 November 2004).

[15] *De l'érection et institution de l'Ordre des Religieuses de Nostre-Dame du Mont-Carmel; selon la Réformation de saincte Térèse en France: des troubles & differends excitez en cet Ordre: & du jugement rendu par nostre sainct Père le Pape sur iceux*. A Messeigneurs les illustrissimes & reverendissimes Cardinaux de La Rochefoucauld & de Retz. Par messire Michel de Marillac, conseiller du Roy en son Conseil d'Estat (Paris: Edme Martin, 1622).

and others in the foundation of the Ursulines in Paris in 1610, and with Pierre de Bérulle in founding the Oratorians in 1611.[16]

We should note the outburst of new and reformed orders taking place in France and elsewhere during these years. To name but two, Saint Jeanne de Lestonnac (1556-1640), a niece of the famous essayist Michel de Montaigne and the widowed baroness of the fabled Château de Landiras, worked closely with Jesuits in Bordeaux to found the Sisters of Notre-Dame (or *La Compagnie de Marie Notre-Dame*) in 1607; and Saint Jeanne de Chantal (1572-1641), who worked alongside Saint François de Sales in founding the Order of the Visitation (or *La Visitation Sainte-Marie*) in 1610. François de Sales (1567-1622), the so-called bishop of Geneva, advised the Acarie circle during his lengthy visit to Paris in 1602. In 1609, he wrote the widely influential *Introduction à la vie dévote*. Jeanne de Chantal was initially attracted to the Carmel in Dijon, and it should be mentioned that Vincent de Paul knew her well and regarded her as "one of the holiest people [he had] ever met on this earth."[17]

I mention these two foundations in particular because of their resemblance to the Daughters of Charity, later founded by Louise de Marillac and Vincent de Paul. All three focussed on providing concrete aid, succor, and instruction in salvation to the sick, poor, and orphaned, as well as vocational education for girls aimed at facilitating their survival in the secular world. In contrast, Louise's uncle devoted his principal efforts to support of the Carmelites, a contemplative order seeking retreat from the world. While my studies have turned up virtually no evidence that Michel de Marillac was much concerned with questions of poverty or social suffering, except in the abstract or as broad political policy,[18] he does appear to have developed a capacity for mysticism through his frequent involvement with

---

[16] The extraordinarily saintly and energetic Barbe Avrillot (1566-1618) was beatified in 1791. Married in 1582 to Pierre Acarie, and widowed in 1613, she then followed three of their daughters into the Carmelite sisterhood, taking the name Marie de l'Incarnation. Her cousin, Pierre de Bérulle (1575-1629), was named a cardinal two years before his death; ordained as a priest in 1599, he was appointed one of the original three Superiors for the French reformed Carmelites, along with André Duval and Jacques Gallemant.

[17] Quoted in Donald Attwater, *The Penguin Dictionary of Saints*, 2nd ed., rev. and updated by Catherine Rachel John (Harmondsworth, Middlesex: Penguin Books, 1983), p. 180.

[18] For example, among Marillac's arguments in favoring political reform over an expanded war was a potential amelioration of the poor's tax burdens. Although some scholars have described this aspect of the *dévot* program as a financial aspiration of the noble class, whose feudal dues could increase if taxes were reduced, I have found no evidence of such *dévot* cynicism / calculation. The *dévots/dévotes* may have been naive and patronizing, but selfishness was not apparent in their activities.

the pious Carmelites.[19] Whatever Louise may have learned from him, she significantly enhanced.

So, now let us consider Louise de Marillac and her uncle together. It is obvious that the extended Marillac family made exceptional contributions to French society for well over a century, in both political and religious institutions and activities. The family context into which Louise was born would lead us to expect the same piety, energy, and administrative capacity that indeed we find in her. And yet, her life might well have missed such fulfillment, for her childhood and youth were hardly settled or secure. She may even have been troubled throughout her life with doubts concerning her own baptism.[20]

Scholars have largely cleared up the mysteries surrounding her birth, but an innocent search in genealogical reference works reveals a variety of sometimes rather wild claims.[21] Her father was Michel's elder full brother, Louis de Marillac, *seigneur de Ferrières-en-Brie, Capitaine des gendarmes de la Maison du Roi*, and / or *Conseiller au Parlement de Paris*. Her mother was Marguerite Le Camus, with whom Louis had a liaison between two marriages. Louis never denied his responsibility, but there is no mention of her mother's having remained in Louise's life at all, nor even any mention of step-mothering — a benefit her uncle Michel most likely had enjoyed himself. On the eve of his remarriage in 1595, her father placed the scarcely four-year-old Louise with the Dominican nuns at Poissy, among whom an aunt was a prominent member.[22] Louis de Marillac moved his natural

---

[19] Jean-Baptiste Eriau writes that the religiously observant life of the Carmelites ("ascetic and mystical") deepened the spiritual life of both Acarie and Marillac (his especially, as he had further to go). Marillac was rapidly initiated "into all the secrets of the interior life" by them. He organized "his household as a sort of monastery and communicated to his family and associates [aux siens] his own spiritual tastes." His letters to Mother Magdeleine de Saint-Joseph show an intense interior life. Eriau, *L'Ancien Carmel du faubourg Saint-Jacques* (Paris: J. de Gigord & A. Picard, 1929), 465 + note 1.

[20] This possibility was related to me in a private conversation (9 March 1999) with Professor Bernard Barbiche of the École des Chartes. One must wonder, however, whether the two dates suggested for Louise's birth (15 March 1591, at Ferrières-en-Brie, in the Marillac's native province of Auvergne, or 12 August, in Paris) suggest that the second was, rather, her date of baptism. Yet, it has been asserted that she was baptized in Ferrières-en-Brie *before* being taken to Paris. See, http://missel.free.fr/Sanctoral/03/15.php (p. 2, accessed 12 July 2010). However, it remains possible that what scholars have claimed was not known to a girl whose early years were so unstable.

[21] Most of both the established and fanciful details, and their sources, can be found in the Genealogical Appendix to my transcription / edition of Lezeau's *Vie de Marillac*. Although I have encountered more examples since, I shall not attempt to present them here.

[22] Many genealogists designate the two Louises as aunt and niece, even though the elder was in fact the aunt of the younger's father. See, for example: http://www.filles-de-la-charite.org/fr/st_louise_de_marillac.aspx (accessed 12 July 2010).

daughter to a more modest accommodation some seven years later, in 1602, and then, on 25 July 1604, he died. Uncle Michel now became the guardian of his approximately thirteen-year-old niece and her younger half-sister.

Thus, in the opening decade of the new century, the royal bureaucrat and religious reformer Michel de Marillac found himself the guardian of at least three nieces: Saint Louise, her less than three-year-old half-sister Innocente de Marillac, and, perhaps a few years later, Catherine du Plessis, a niece of Marillac's through his second wife Marie de Saint-Germain (married 1601). Marillac had himself been orphaned at the same age as Louise, and so might have been expected to empathize with the fate of his nieces. On Innocente's sixth birthday (1607), Marillac put her, along with his own daughter Valence (now about eight years old) — no mention of Louise here! — into the newly established Ursuline convent in Paris.[23] I am not aware that we know very much about Michel and Louise's interactions during this period. But it may be instructive to note, that, once Louise achieved adulthood, their subsequent correspondence reveals very little personal interaction between uncle and niece.[24] What is known is that Saint Louise was erudite, devout, and spiritually quite sensitive, and in these respects she reflected her uncle's attributes at a similar age.

The respectable marriage Louise entered into, despite her inclinations towards a religious life, probably served the ambitions of the half-brothers Michel and Louis de Marillac as much as it provided her social standing and security. Louise's proposed husband was Antoine Le Gras (ca. 1577-1625), private secretary (*secrétaire des commandements*) of Marie de Medici, the Queen Mother. Nonetheless, on 18 October 1613, a son, Michel-Antoine, was born to the couple some eight months after their marriage, and they appear to have been happy. Madame Le Gras's spiritual crises, however, continued to torment her, despite the interventions of François de Sales and

---

[23] In 1617, Innocente married Jean d'Aspremont, sgr de Vandy. They were to have one daughter, Catherine de Vandy (1620-1685), who became a *fille d'honneur* to the "Grande Mademoiselle." Marie-Andrée Jégou, O.S.U., *Les Ursulines du Faubourg Saint-Jacques à Paris (1607-1662). Origine d'un monastère apostolique* (Paris: Presses Universitaires de France, 1981), 19, and note 30; among others.

[24] Jean-Dominique Mellot, *Histoire du Carmel de Pontoise, I, 1605-1792* (Paris: Desclée de Brouwer, 1994), 20, note 5.

Nonetheless, if it is true that after 1619 Madame Le Gras (Louise) and her husband took charge of the seven orphans of her father's widowed half-sister,* Valence de Marillac-Dony (d. 1617), and her husband Octavien II Dony d'Attichy (d. 1614), Louise would have shared this responsibility with her uncle Michel, who was also involved in their well-being and education.

* See, http://missel.free.fr/Sanctoral/03/15.php (p. 2, accessed 12 July 2010). It should also be noted that Louise's marriage was proposed not only by her two uncles, but by the husband of this aunt, the same Octavien II Dony d'Attichy, who was equally interested in strengthening his political connections. See, http://fr.wikipedia.org.wiki/Louise (p. 2, accessed 12 July 2010). However, he died the year after the marriage.

others in 1619. Perhaps because of a pre-mature birth, Michel-Antoine was never robust, and then his father fell gravely ill in 1622. The latter died on 21 December 1625, leaving Louise a wealthy widow.[25] By this time, she had already encountered Vincent de Paul, who took over Louise's spiritual direction towards the end of 1624.

Apart from providing context to Louise and Michel's interrelationships, it is not my concern, of course, to present Louise de Marillac's life, let alone the extraordinary partnership forged over the next 35 years with Vincent de Paul. It suffices, I hope, to reiterate that we know little about her direct interactions with her uncle. It is quite probable that he responsibly looked after her material needs, her educational and spiritual development, though without being any closer or warmer to her than he was to anyone else. In any case, during the period of her marriage and early widowhood Michel was phenomenally preoccupied with affairs of state.

Engraving of Cardinal Richelieu (1582-1642).
By Robert Nanteuil, 1657. Collection of the Yale University Art Gallery.
Public Domain

---

[25] Specific information about the marriage and family, some of which I had not previously encountered, comes from Comte de Lambel, *La Bienheureuse Louise de Marillac (Mademoiselle Le Gras) Co-fondatrice de la Compagnie des Filles de la Charité* (Paris-Lille: A. Taffin-Lefort, 1919), 218 p.: marriage on 5 February 1613 (p. 23); Michel-Antoine born on 19 October 1613 (Lambel says only "dès la fin de l'année," p. 32); widowed 21 December 1625 (p. 34); son's marriage in 1650 to Gabrielle le Clerc, daughter of sgr. de Chenevières, and one daughter born (pp. 32-3).

Others, however, describe her financial position as "precarious," though perhaps to emphasize her saintly generosity in donating at least part of her wealth to Saint-Nicolas du Chardonnet. For example, http://fr.wikipedia.org.wiki/Louise (p. 2, accessed 12 July 2010).

One scholar does, however, speak of her "retiring from Court" in 1625.[26] This suggests that, before widowhood, she had been participating in the social life expected of women of her status, a responsibility quite likely reinforced by her uncle's (and no doubt her husband's) political ambitions. With her uncle's disgrace and death during the fledgling years of the Daughters of Charity, both discretion and her own challenging preoccupations undoubtedly kept niece and uncle personally apart.

Cardinal Richelieu, with royal sanction, treated the two Marillac half-brothers brutally after the Day of Dupes (10-11 November 1630); coincidentally, the wife of the *maréchal*, and the Capuchin son of the *garde des sceaux* died at about the same time. The Queen Mother herself suffered exile from France. One has to wonder how this affected others closely attached to these rivals. It is thus noteworthy that Richelieu's own niece, Madame d'Aiguillon (marquise de Combalet), a friend to both the Carmelites and later to the Daughters of Charity, helped Marillac's daughter-in-law circumvent the Cardinal's attempts to hinder funeral arrangements. Meanwhile François Sublet des Noyers, a royal councilor close to both Marillac and the Carmelites, was soon to be made Minister of War on Richelieu's recommendation. Vincent de Paul himself seems not to have come under suspicion for his associations with other leading *dévots*, nor was his work hindered in any way. It also appears that Louise de Marillac's life and activities in these crucial, fertile years similarly suffered no impediments that could be ascribed to Richelieu's suspicions or animosities. Nor do other Marillac relations appear to have had their careers interrupted.[27]

What I hope has been both interesting and of use in this article, however, is a richer understanding of the extraordinary family from which Louise de Marillac emerged — and especially of the life and career of her equally noteworthy uncle. Despite the obscurity and dishonor surrounding her birth, Louise appears to have received the same sustenance and education as that of her legitimate half-sister and her cousins, and to have benefitted

---

[26] Jean-François Dubost, "Une Reine et une Capitale Catholiques," part of "Reine, Régente, Reine Mère," in *Marie de Médicis et le Palais de Luxembourg*, éd. Marie-Noëlle Baudouin-Matuszek (Paris: Délégation à l'Action Artistique de la Ville de Paris, 1991), p. 143.

[27] This fact contrasts strongly, for instance, with the fate of Nicolas Lefèvre de Lezeau's (Marillac biographer) grandnephews after their father had unexpectedly frustrated Louis XIV's desires for a quick and severe judgment against Nicolas Fouquet (1615-1680), his recently disgraced finance minister. The vigorous defense of his former colleague by Olivier III Lefèvre d'Ormesson (1616-1686) probably saved Fouquet's life — but it ended Ormesson's own career and delayed those of his sons. Jean-François Solnon, *Les Ormesson au plaisir de l'État* ([Paris]: Fayard, 1992), pp. 103-31; also Solon's article in François Bluche, *Dictionnaire du Grand Siècle*. One must soften one's censure of Richelieu from time to time and admire his perspicacity in judging competence and loyalty.

throughout her life and career from such advantages. These advantages both contrasted with those experienced by Vincent de Paul in his youth, yet complemented the capacities he brought to the enterprises of his later life. Furthermore, Michel de Marillac stood out from almost all his lay colleagues for his exceptional spiritual devotion, and for the energy and generosity he brought to the French Catholic Reformation. In her uncle and guardian, especially, and not simply the Marillac family in general, Louise de Marillac had a model of devout practice and spiritual commitment that undoubtedly contributed profoundly to her own. Perhaps it is appropriate that, today, they are both emerging from the shadows.

Pictures from the Past:
The First University of Dallas

By

Stafford Poole, C.M.[1]

Facing view of the University of Dallas.
Courtesy of DeAndreis-Rosati Memorial Archives, DePaul University Special Collections, Chicago, IL

Of all the institutions of higher learning inaugurated and conducted by the Vincentian Community, none has a more appalling or tragic history than the University of Dallas.

Like so many of the others, it was undertaken at the request of the ordinary, in this case Edward Dunne (1848-1910), the second bishop of Dallas. Having known the work of the Vincentians when he was a diocesan priest in Chicago, he was eager to have them in his diocese. His offer of a college and parish was accepted first by Father Thomas Smith and then by Father William Barnwell on behalf of the Western Province in 1905. A short time later twenty-four acres of wooded land were purchased in the north of the city for $20,000.

---

[1] The following is an excerpt from *The American Vincentians: A Popular History of the Congregation of the Mission in the United States, 1815-1987*, ed. John E. Rybolt, C.M. (Brooklyn, N.Y.: New City Press, 1988), pp. 329-338. The book is available for purchase online at http://vsi.depaul.edu, click on Printed Resources, then Bookstore; or inquire by phone at 312-362-7139.

106

The construction of Holy Trinity College — later named the University of Dallas.
Courtesy DeAndreis-Rosati Memorial Archives, DePaul University Special Collections, Chicago, IL

Postcard. Holy Trinity College (Holy Trinity Catholic Church at left). Printed by Grombach-Faisans Co., New Orleans, LA, circa 1908.

Postcard. Scene near the Holy Trinity College, Dallas, TX. Circa 1909.

Images courtesy of Vincentiana Collection, DePaul University Special Collections, Chicago, IL

Barnwell and the provincial council were determined that the Vincentian entry into the new venture would be a cautious one. It was decided that $40,000 would be raised by loans from the houses of the provinces, another $40,000 in a fund-raising campaign, and a final $20,000 would be borrowed on the land and furnishings of the college. At least one house, Saint Stephen's in New Orleans, refused to make the loan.

Father Patrick Finney was appointed the first superior and president. One of four brothers who were priests in the Congregation of the Mission, he was a man of boundless, and sometimes variable, enthusiasms but lacked a good managerial style. His theoretical grasp of financial practice was good, his execution was not. After his arrival in Dallas, he was told by a group of local businessmen that the plans for the school were entirely too small and that they would raise $25,000, a promise that was never kept. Finney accepted this at face value and committed the province to pay the $100,000 for building a school twice the size of what was originally planned. Barnwell was aghast and rebuked Finney sharply. Two months later Barnwell died.

His successor was Father Thomas Finney, Patrick Finney's older brother. This proved disastrous because it removed whatever restraint there was on Patrick Finney. For the next eleven years he was a free agent, with the result that both the college and the province were caught in an ever mounting spiral of debt. In order to finance the construction of the college building, Patrick Finney entered into a complex agreement with a Chicago-based insurance company (which had also lent money to DePaul University). The deal ran into trouble almost immediately when the insurer tried to change the terms of the agreement, failed to forward payments, and finally went out of business altogether. Before doing so, it sold Finney's debts to a number of banks.

At Dunne's suggestion, the new school was called Holy Trinity College, and it opened in September 1907. It was housed in a magnificent building four stories high and with a southern façade of 370 feet. It was at first only a high school, with an opening enrollment of eighty-eight which rose to 160 by 1910. During its first years the college was beset by numerous problems, including a recession, a drought, and an outbreak of illness. American entrance into World War I hurt it still more by draining off students and faculty.

Priests at the back entrance to the
University of Dallas, dated May 1918.
Pictured are, bottom row:
Charles McCarthy, Thomas Powers, Thomas
Levan, Walter Quinn; middle row: Manuel
de Françaises, Richard Delonly, Walter Case;
top row: Edward Fuller, Peter Finnly, Thomas
Reynolds, John Le Doge.

Classes at the University of Dallas,
no date.

University of Dallas pennant, includes official seal.

*Images courtesy of DeAndreis-Rosati Memorial Archives,
DePaul University Special Collections, Chicago, IL*

The worst blow was the death of Bishop Dunne in 1910. His successor was Joseph Lynch, the first Episcopal alumnus of Kenrick Seminary in Saint Louis, who was bishop from 1911 to 1954. Whereas Dunne had been an active supporter of the college, Lynch was indifferent to it. He offered little or no support, would not help it in its financial difficulties but insisted on holding the Vincentians to the letter of their contract with the diocese.

Supposedly it was at the suggestion of Bishop Dunne that the name of the school was changed to the University of Dallas in 1910 in order to prevent that name from being appropriated by a group of non-Catholics. In theory this meant that it could now offer collegiate courses in the proper sense. By 1915 three primary grades had been added for the sake of students from rural areas, and there was a smattering of students on the junior college level. In 1916 the university granted an M.A. and in 1917 an unearned Ph.D. degree to its vice president, Father Marshall Winne.

One of the principal problems was Patrick Finney's disorganized administration. He was absent from the university for long periods, insisted on doing all important things himself, and kept poor records. Worst of all, however, was the debt. The deficit for the year 1909 was $30,000, and the total debt, insofar as it was known, was $296,056. No financial records exist from the Finney years, perhaps because his personal papers were destroyed by his brothers after his death. One of Finney's schemes for making money, turning the college laundry into a commercial one, backfired and cost the college more money than it made. Another scheme, purchasing and developing a tract of land called Loma Linda, was sound in theory but, as will be seen later, failed in practice.

In 1917 Patrick Finney suffered a breakdown and was hospitalized for almost a year. Father Marshall Winne, the vice president, took over the day-to-day operation of the university. Because there had already been hints of trouble, the provincial council named Father Thomas Levan as president pro tem (while at the same time he remained superior of Saint Vincent's College in Cape Girardeau) and sent him to Dallas to investigate the situation.

Levan's report was a shock to the council and, apparently, to the provincial. The University of Dallas had a debt of over $700,000 and a yearly deficit of $25,000 to $30,000. The council sent Levan to inform Bishop Lynch of the situation and seek his help. Both the bishop, and later his consulters, rebuffed the Vincentians. Levan recommended to the council that the university be closed and its assets sold to satisfy its creditors. This was rejected both by the council and by Bishop Lynch, who insisted that the Vincentians fulfill the contract under which they had come to Dallas.

With the province on the brink of bankruptcy, Charles Souvay wrote to the superior general in Paris, that the provincial and his council had known nothing of the Dallas debt. "It was, then, from top to bottom a reign of an inconceivable incoherence." He concluded:

> The Visitor [provincial] does not seem to realize that his brother was of such inconceivable disorder and extravagance in his administration; that he is, materially, gravely responsible for the disaster of that house and directly of the province. I dare say that his sickness has been providential. Otherwise we would most likely still be in ignorance of the precipice that he has dug under our feet. And I would dare to add that the most efficacious measures should be taken to make sure that M. Patrick Finney, if he lives a hundred years, will never again be appointed a superior.[2]

As acting president of Dallas, Levan struggled to find some way to extricate the university from its debts. Unknown to him, Thomas Finney and the council were planning to appoint him permanent president of the university in the hope that, once faced with the accomplished fact, he would accept the position. Word leaked out, however, and Levan loudly opposed the plan. As Thomas Finney admitted, "it was to demand heroism."[3] The mantle of heroism was thereupon given to Father Marshall Winne (October 1918). Both the university and the province were given a reprieve in the form of a $200,000 loan from the Daughters of Charity.

Father Winne's term of office (1918-1922) was difficult and frustrating. A long-anticipated fund drive was undertaken. Bishop Lynch refused to write a supporting letter until a committee of laypersons, including some influential protestants, persuaded him to do so. His letter (9 February 1919) was notable for its lack of enthusiasm. Many of the diocesan clergy were actively hostile to the drive. It was an overall failure. In 1920 the primary school grades were discontinued. Efforts to draw more students by means of scholarships simply lowered the income available from tuition.

One of Winne's crosses was the university's treasurer, Father Hugh O'Connor. O'Connor was constantly dabbling in various schemes to rescue the university, including a fund-raising campaign in the diocese of Galveston that he undertook without the bishop's permission. Worse still

---

[2] Souvay to Verdier, 28 May 1918, Microfilm of American materials (to 1935) in the Archives of the General Curia, Rome: series D, roll 2.
[3] Finney to Verdier, 1 April 1918, DeAndreis-Rosati Memorial Archives, DePaul University, Chicago, IL (DRMA), Finney papers.

111

The auditorium and dance hall.

Students pose at dining table.

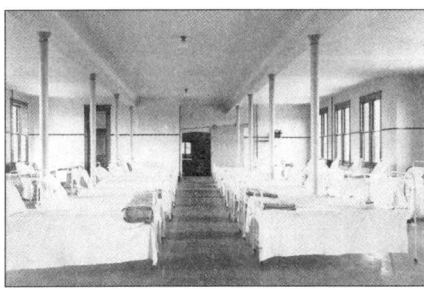

The dormitory.

The chemical lab.

*Images courtesy of DeAndreis-Rosati Memorial Archives,
DePaul University Special Collections, Chicago, IL*

112

Postcard. Holy Trinity College.
Printed by The Albertype Co., Brooklyn, New York.
Handwritten note at bottom reads:
"RC thinks this is the only school on earth."
Courtesy of Vincentiana Collection, DePaul University Special Collections, Chicago, IL

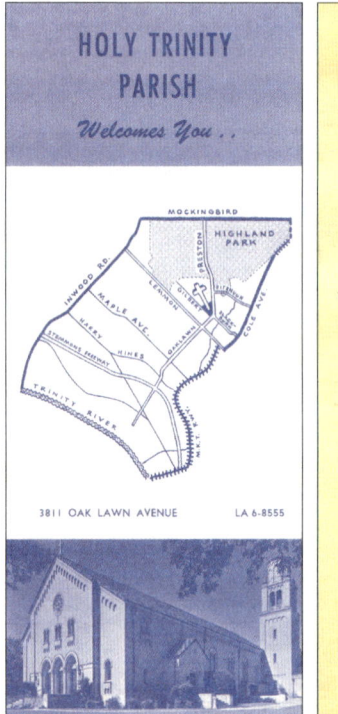

At left, parish brochure (mid-twentieth century) including map of grounds which housed the University of Dallas. At right, a homecoming program for the University of Dallas, undated.
Courtesy of DeAndreis-Rosati Memorial Archives, DePaul University Special Collections, Chicago, IL

was his involvement with a shady oilman named J.J. O'Malley. In February 1922 O'Connor sent out letters of solicitation, inviting people to invest in O'Malley's drilling activities, with the university receiving one-fourth of the profits. O'Connor's letter quoted a number of prominent Dallas businessmen in support of the venture. Unfortunately these endorsements were either false or exaggerated. O'Malley was eventually arrested for mail fraud, and the university suffered a great deal of embarrassment. Winne wrote to Thomas Finney, "I am absolutely discouraged and disgusted."[4] Winne was relieved of his office in June 1922, and O'Connor was transferred to Chicago to become a fund raiser for DePaul University.

After two other candidates had turned down the office, Father William Barr was appointed president. He served for only one year. The reasons for the brevity of this appointment are not known. In August 1923 Father Thomas Powers was named to succeed him. He set out to reinvigorate the university, especially by introducing coeducation. This project failed, probably because of opposition by Bishop Lynch. Powers also secured a "Class A" rating for the university from the Association of Texas Colleges. While it brought prestige, it also required that a minimum enrollment be maintained and that college and high school faculties be kept separate. This, in turn, demanded more financial outlay.

Powers lasted only two years. In 1925 he was removed for reasons that are not now clear. Thomas Finney gave a number of excuses, none of which was entirely convincing. In September 1925 the provincial and his council appointed Father Walter Quinn as president but two months later named him director of novices at Saint Mary's Seminary in Perryville, Missouri. Father Thomas Carney succeeded him. The University of Dallas thus had the dubious distinction of having had three presidents within one year, a fact that was not lost on Bishop Lynch or the people of Dallas.

Carney was young, thirty-three, and talented but also of a sensitive and moody nature. The university was to be a calamitous experience for him, in part because Patrick Finney returned to Dallas in order to salvage it. In 1908 Finney had purchased some choice property, later called Loma Linda, which he now proposed to develop. In 1924 and 1925 he secured his brother's permission to proceed with the development himself. Barr, then the superior at the Barrens, heard about this and sent letters to the provincial consultors, begging them to rein in Finney and stop the project. His efforts failed. Finney again acted as an independent agent and was able to speak for the university without being attached to it. He formed a group of advisors and investors and within a short time the first tract, called Section I, was

---

[4] Winne to Finney, 22 March 1922, DRMA, Finney papers.

completed and incorporated as part of the suburb called University Park. Almost immediately the bottom fell out of the Dallas real estate market, with values declining by 13 to 30 percent. Within a year the Loma Linda project had a debt of $465,430.

Carney chafed under a situation he could not control. It changed dramatically in March 1926 when Thomas Finney resigned as provincial and, after Michael Ryan's refusal of the post, Barr succeeded him. Carney took advantage of the change of administration to assert his authority over Loma Linda and to remove Patrick Finney. The two had a loud confrontation at the university, but Carney prevailed. Carney then was able to persuade Edward Doheny of Los Angeles (whom Carney had known when he was an assistant at Saint Vincent's parish) to pay the interest on the university's debt. In 1926 he eliminated the senior college program, the boarding students, and the athletic program.

In March 1927 as the banks began to close in on the university, Carney suffered a nervous breakdown. Barr, Levan, and the provincial council again turned to Doheny who assumed the university's debt on which he would hold bonds for ten years. It was not a donation because the province was obliged to repay him at the end of that period. Shortly thereafter the province was able to sell the remaining Loma Linda property, and the university's debts had been temporarily settled.

All of this was too late to help Carney. Barr was hostile to Carney, whose appointment he had opposed, and was insensitive to the young man's sufferings. In July 1927 he summarily removed him as president. Carney was shocked, and when he hinted that he might appeal to the superior general, Barr forestalled him by writing a generic letter of denunciation filled with vague charges and innuendos. In August Carney asked for his release from the Community and after being forced to wait for several months, was granted it. He entered the diocese of Galveston where he became a pastor and monsignor and gained a nationwide reputation as a speaker on radio's Catholic Hour. He died in Texas on 1 November 1950. The whole procedure reflects little credit on Barr.

The next, and last, president of the University of Dallas was Father Charles McCarthy. The college department was now completely eliminated, and only the high school remained. In May 1928 Barr and his council determined to close even that and extricate the province from its last involvement with the university. He informed Lynch of the decision but received no answer. A second letter conveyed again the decision not to reopen the high school in September 1929. Lynch then began a strange, last ditch campaign to save the high school, but it was too little and too late. In a letter bristling with indignation, Barr announced the final withdrawal

115

The woodshop.

The gymnasium.

A student's room.

Images courtesy of DeAndreis-Rosati Memorial Archives, DePaul University Special Collections, Chicago, IL

but emphasized that the Vincentians would retain the parish (the present Holy Trinity), which they owned outright. On 1 February 1929 the provincial council reiterated that the province would under no circumstances consider reopening the college.

Still the matter was not ended. At the end of 1928 Barr had to deal with an anonymous denunciation to Rome of the Vincentians and their work in Dallas. It almost certainly seems to have been the work of Bishop Lynch. Barr responded with a strong and lengthy statement, and nothing was heard of the denunciations again, perhaps because the demise of the university was by then an accomplished fact.

The bad management of the University of Dallas continued to the end in the disposition of the property. After some other offers for the land and building had fallen through, Lynch offered to assume the current debt of $157,000 and take the land. The offer was accepted, and on 27 May 1929 McCarthy signed a formal transfer to Lynch with a restrictive covenant that it could be used for white people only. What McCarthy omitted or forgot to tell Lynch was that he had let out an option to some other buyers, who now sued to gain control of the property. Lynch demanded and obtained from the province security against possible loss. The courts awarded the land to the second group of buyers on condition that they raise sufficient money to pay for it. When they failed to do so, it reverted to Lynch.

The bishop had intended to use the building for a diocesan high school, but in 1930 a girls' orphanage moved into the building. In 1941 the Jesuits opened a high school and three years later purchased the property from Lynch for about the same amount that he paid for it. In 1963 they sold it for a handsome profit and used the money to build a new high school elsewhere. Within two years the original building had been torn down. The Western Province vacated the title University of Dallas in 1954 and the present institution of that name has no organic connection with the one directed by the Vincentians.

In retrospect it can be seen that the University of Dallas was doomed to failure from the beginning. There were not enough local resources to support a college, much less a university. In 1905 Dallas was a small city with a small Catholic population. The project was launched on an extravagant scale and on the basis of a misunderstanding about the province's financial responsibility. Patrick Finney had many winning qualities, especially in the field of public relations, but he was not suited to be the chief executive officer of an academic institution. The top level of administration was characterized by great instability: between 1917 and 1929 there were six different presidents. Once the province had been committed to the university,

Students assembled in the dining room.
Courtesy of DeAndreis-Rosati Memorial Archives, DePaul University Special Collections, Chicago, IL

Postcard. Holy Trinity College. Printed by S.H. Kress & Co., postmarked 1917.
Courtesy of Vincentiana Collection, DePaul University Special Collections, Chicago, IL

there was great reluctance to admit failure and withdraw. The unhappy coincidence that the two Finney brothers were president and provincial was damaging to both the university and the province and made any admission of failure highly unlikely.

Extrinsic factors, such as recessions, drought, epidemics, and the collapse of the real estate market worsened an already bad situation. The hostile, or at best indifferent, attitude of Bishop Lynch was another negative factor. His reluctance to become financially involved in such a venture was quite understandable. His insistence on holding the province to the letter of the contract was not.

The University of Dallas was a classic example of throwing good money after bad. Unfortunately, in its descent it almost carried the province with it. This was clear to many, such as Levan, who strongly advised severing the Community's involvement with it. In 1918 one of his confreres wrote to him that attempts to maintain the university were "throwing money at the birds. There is no power on earth that can make the University of Dallas succeed and I do not see the sense of going deeper into debt."[5] Unfortunately such advice was not heeded, and the province skirted the edge of disaster.

University of Dallas bronze plaque with official seal.
Courtesy of DeAndreis-Rosati Memorial Archives, DePaul University Special Collections, Chicago, IL

---

[5] Martin Hanley to Levan, 4 February 1918, DRMA, University of Dallas papers.

NEWSNOTES

NEWS

Beatification of Marguerite Rutan, D.C.
On 1 July 2010, Pope Benedict XVI approved the recognition of the martyrdom of Sister Marguerite Rutan, D.C., at Dax in 1793 during the French Revolution. Her beatification is set to take place in Dax in the spring of 2011.

Debut of *Vincentian History Research Network* (VHRN)
The DePaul University Vincentian Studies Institute is proud to announce the debut of the *Vincentian History Research Network* (VHRN) — a dynamic online forum designed for researchers and scholars to discuss Vincentian topics broadly considered.

The VHRN is an online network where participants can learn about Vincentian resources, share current research projects, ask questions about possible archival and bibliographic resources, announce publications or upcoming conferences, and seek grant funding.

Those interested are invited to view and/or join the forum at:

http://vhrn-depaul.ning.com/

It is hoped that the VHRN will aid in creating a worldwide community of "Vincentian" scholars. As many scholars are multi-lingual, all languages are welcome.

PUBLICATIONS

BOOKS

Jack Melito, C.M., *Saint Vincent de Paul: His Mind and His Manner* (Chicago: DePaul University Vincentian Studies Institute, 2010), 127 pp.

From promotional materials: "This new work by Father Melito follows in the tradition of his popular *Saint Vincent de Paul: Windows on His Vision*. It features over thirty poignant essays and prayers on a wide variety of topics relevant to our Vincentian Family. The title itself, *His Mind and His Manner*, suggests something in St. Vincent's writing which is more than conventional address. The Saint said many things to his varied audiences, elaborating upon his beliefs, his teachings, and his spirituality — his "mind," if you will. His "manner" derived from the informal mode employed in his conferences, addressing his communities in a personal tone. Together, as reflected upon within these pages, these features of Vincent's voice shed greater light on the Saint's personality."

John Rybolt, C.M., *The Vincentians: A General History of the Congregation of the Mission. Volume One: 1625-1697* (Hyde Park, N.Y.: New City Press, 2009), 394 pp.

From promotional materials: "For the first time, modern readers have a thoroughly researched history based on original documents and the studies of numerous scholars, past and present. It portrays the Vincentians' daily lives and describes their failings as well as their exalted acts of heroism. It also details the social and political milieus that conditioned their lives and work. It is an important, down-to-earth side of history not often told.

Each book in the six volume series focuses upon the general government of the Congregation, including chapters on individual provinces, and each contains maps and several illustrations. Supplemental text will be available online, courtesy of DePaul University's *Via Sapientiae* website: http://via.library.depaul.edu/histories

Volume one, written by Luigi Mezzadri, C.M., and the late José María Román, C.M., is now available in English for the first time. Volume 2, by Luigi Mezzadri, C.M., and Francesca Onnis, on the History of the Congregation up to the French Revolution, 1789, will be released in English in 2011. The remaining volumes, authored by John Rybolt, C.M., will be published in subsequent years."

JOURNALS

Anales de la Congregación de la Misión y de las Hijas de la Caridad. Mayo-Junio, Vol. 118:3 (2010), "Papers from the *Congres de la Familia Vincenciana* held in Madrid, 5-7 March 2010," includes:
- Luis Gonzales-Carvajal Santabarbara, "La fe de Vicente de Paúl ante una sociedad de increencia."
- Patricia P. de Nava, "La experiencia spiritual y caritativa de Vicente de Paúl."
- Benito Martinez, C.M., "La fe de Santa Luisa ante una sociedad individualista."
- María Ángeles Infante, D.C., "La experiencia ecclesial y caritativa de Santa Luisa de Marillac, ayer y hoy."

Noviembre-Diciembre, Vol. 118:6 (2010), includes:
- Joaquin Gonzalez, C.M., "La sensibilidad de San Vicente de Paúl cuajada en lagrimas."

Cahiers Saint Vincent: Bulletin des Lazaristes de France, Revue trimestrielle de la Congrégation de la Mission en France, Numero 211 (Été 2010), features:
- Bernard Massarini, C.M., "Monsieur Vincent ou le sacerdoce avec le Christ Evangelisateur des Pauvres."

Numero 212 (Automne 2010), "'Vincent de Paul et Louise de Marillac aujourd'hui' Actes du Colloque 15-15 Mai 2010, au Berceau de Saint-Vincent-de-Paul," includes:
- Philippe Molac, P.S.S., "La Formation Théologique de Vincent de Paul, Fondement de la Mission de Charité," pp. 15-24.

Carità e Missione: Rivista di studi e formazione vincenziana. Published by the Italian provinces of the Congregation of the Mission and the Daughters of Charity.

Anno X, Number 1 (2010), dedicated to the Vincentian jubilee year, features:
- Jean-Pierre Renouard, C.M., "L'esperienza umana e spirituale di Santa Luisa de Marillac."
- Giiovanni Burdese, C.M., "Magistero pontificio su Santa Luisa de Marillac."
- Antonella Ponte, F.d.C., "Luisa de Marillac. I poveri sorgente di forza nella carita."
- Salvatore Fari, C.M., "Leggere Luisa de Marillac fra rigore organizzativo e abbandono allo Spirito d'Amore, Giulia Oteri Vincenzianesimo ed azione educative."
- Paola Pizzi, F.d.C., "Esplorando il cuore di una madre."
- Maria Rosaria Matranga, F.d.C., "Luisa de Marillac patrona degli operatori sociali."
- Assunta Corona, F.d.C., "Carita e giustizia in Santa Luisa: ieri e oggi."
- Nunzia De Gori, S.d.C., "La silenziosa rivoluzione di Jeanne-Antide Thouret a Napoli. A 200 anni... memoria di una fondazione!"

Anno X, Number 2 (2010), also dedicated to the Vincentian jubilee year, features:
- Benito Martiez, C.M., "Vincenzo e Luisa: una fedelta creative e audace."
- Elisabeth Charpy, D.C., "Luisa de Marillac animatrice delle Confraternite della Carita."
- Alberto Vernaschi, C.M., "Umanizzazione del servizio di autorita in San Vincenzo e Santa Luisa."
- Enrique Rivas Vila, C.M., "Cinque volti di P. Portail."
- Antonio Furioli, M.C.C.J., "Il frutto piu prezioso dell'apostolato missionario di San Giustino de Jacobis. Il Beato Gabra Mika'el (1791-1855), martire per la fede in Abissinia."
- Alberto Vernaschi, C.M., "Vincenzo e Luisa e la Carita di Gesu crocifisso."

The Catholic Historical Review, Vol. XCVI, No. 4 (October 2010), includes:
- Douglas J. Slawson, "The Ordeal of Abram J. Ryan (1860-1863)."

Echoes of the Company: The monthly international magazine of the Company of the Daughters of Charity.

Issue Number 2, March-April 2010, includes:
- Claire Hermann, D.C., "Louise de Marillac in Her Times."
- Benito Martinez, C.M., "The joint influence of Vincent de Paul and Louise de Marillac on the nature of the Company."

Issue Number 3, May-June 2010, No. 3, features:
- Claire Hermann, D.C., "Louise de Marillac: Organizer."
- Benito Martinez, C.M., "The spirituality of Saint Vincent and Saint Louise."

Vincentiana: This magazine of the Congregation of the Mission is published every two months by the General Curia in Rome.

Volume 54, No. 1, January-March 2010, contains the following articles of interest:
- Corpus Juan Delgado Rubio, C.M., "'Apostolic Men.' A priest from the Perspective of Vincent de Paul's Experience."
- Patrick J. Griffin, C.M., "Vincent as Priest: A personal reflection."

Volume 54, No. 2, April-June 2010, entitled 350 Years and the Mission Continues, includes:
- John E. Rybolt, C.M., "'According to our Institute.' The Charter of the Congregation of the Mission."
- Robert P. Maloney, C.M., "Betrand Ducournau."
- Jose Vega Herrera, C.M., "Father Antoine Portail."
- Antonio Furioli, M.C.C.J., "The Eucharist, Manifestation of Dialogue and Communion: as Demonstrated in St. Justin de Jacobis."

A supplement to *Vincentiana* 54:2, April-June 2010, features:
- Bernard Koch, C.M., "M. Vincent Re-Reads his Life or the Interior Man as Seen by Himself."

Vincentian Studies Institute

VINCENTIAN HERITAGE

SUBSCRIPTIONS

The Vincentian Studies Institute publishes semi-annual issues of *Vincentian Heritage* on matters of Vincentian interest and makes them available to members of the Vincentian Family of Saint Vincent de Paul in the United States.

Subscriptions by persons other than the above are available at the rate of $22.00 a year domestic, and $30.00 for international delivery.

Individual copies of previously published issues may be obtained at $12.00 per copy.

In addition to the subscription fee, the Institute also welcomes contributions in support of its ideals and works in the area of research and pertinent publications.

Make checks payable to the DEPAUL UNIVERSITY VINCENTIAN STUDIES INSTITUTE.

Subscription fees and requests for back issues (or contributions) should be sent to:

> Mr. Nathaniel Michaud
> DePaul University Vincentian Studies Institute
> 55 East Jackson Blvd.
> Suite 850F
> Chicago, IL 60604
> nmichaud@depaul.edu

Name: _____

Address: _____
_____
_____
_____

❏ New ❏ Gift ❏ Renewal

Saint Vincent de Paul: His Mind and His Manner

Jack Melito, C.M.

This new work by Father Melito follows in the tradition of his popular *Saint Vincent de Paul: Windows on His Vision*. It features over thirty poignant essays and prayers on a wide variety of topics relevant to our Vincentian Family. The title itself, *His Mind and His Manner*, suggests something in St. Vincent's writing which is more than conventional address. The Saint said many things to his varied audiences, elaborating upon his beliefs, his teachings, and his spirituality — his "mind," if you will. His "manner" derived from the informal mode employed in his conferences, addressing his communities in a personal tone. Together, as reflected upon within these pages, these features of Vincent's voice shed greater light on the Saint's personality.

About the Author
Over the years Father Melito has served in three major apostolates of the Congregation of the Mission's Midwest Province: in college seminaries providing academic and priestly formation; in serving as Provincial Director for the Daughters of Charity; and in parish ministry. His experiences in these venues led him to reflect and write upon topics such as Vincentian history, spirituality, life, and activity. Now in quasi-retirement, Father Melito continues to draw upon these memories and write on similar topics.

Publication Specifics:
Publication Date: January 2011
Page Count: 127
ISBN: 978-1-936696-00-0
Cover Price: $16.00
For more information contact Mr. Nathaniel Michaud of the DePaul University Vincentian Studies Institute at (312) 362-6169 or nmichaud@depaul.edu.

Ordering:
Available online at: http://tinyurl.com/vincentian-bookstore
Or contact Mr. Stan Lohman, DePaul University Barnes & Noble Bookstores, at (773) 325-7767.

Now Vincent – icon of charity, friend to all –
Links those friends in witness everywhere
To give the love of God worldwide a human face.

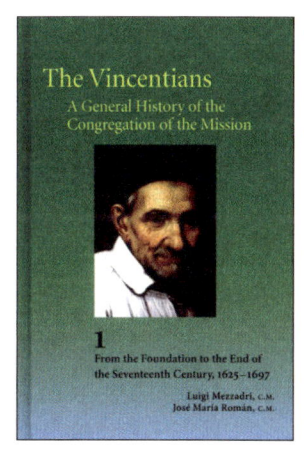

The Vincentians: A General History of the Congregation of the Mission Volume One: 1625-1697

Authors
Luigi Mezzadri, C.M.
José María Román, C.M.

Translated by
Robert Cummings

Edited by
Joseph E. Dunne
John E. Rybolt, C.M.

Summary:
For the first time, modern readers have a thoroughly researched history based on original documents and the studies of numerous scholars, past and present. It portrays the Vincentians' daily lives and describes their failings as well as their exalted acts of heroism. It also details the social and political milieus that conditioned their lives and work. It is an important, down-to-earth side of history not often told.

Each book in the six volume series focuses upon the general government of the Congregation, including chapters on individual provinces, and each contains maps and several illustrations. Supplemental text will be available online, courtesy of DePaul University's *Via Sapientiae* website: http://via.library.depaul.edu/histories

Volume one, written by Luigi Mezzadri, C.M., and the late José María Román, C.M., is now available in English for the first time. Volume 2, by Luigi Mezzadri, C.M., and Francesca Onnis, will be released in English in 2011. The remaining volumes, authored by John Rybolt, C.M., will be published in subsequent years.

Vol. 1: From the Foundation of the Congregation in 1625 to the End of the 17th Century.
Vol. 2: The History of the Congregation up to the French Revolution, 1789.
Vol. 3: The Revolution through the Generalate of Jean-Baptiste Nozo, 1843.
Vol. 4: The Generalates of Jean-Baptiste Étienne and Eugene Boré, 1878.
Vol. 5: The Generalates of Antoine Fiat and Emile Villette, 1919.
Vol. 6: The Generalates from 1919 through 1984.

Publication Specifics:
Publication Date: Volume One, December 2009 (New City Press)
Page Count: 394
ISBN: 978-1-56548-321-7
Cover Price: $39.95
For more information contact Mr. Nathaniel Michaud of the DePaul University Vincentian Studies Institute at (312) 362-6169 or nmichaud@depaul.edu.

Ordering:
Available online at: http://tinyurl.com/thevincentians
Or contact Mr. Stan Lohman, DePaul University Barnes & Noble Bookstores, at (773) 325-7767.